THE GOOD STRESS GUIDE

MARY HARTLEY was born in London and brought up in Weybridge, Surrey. After a career in teaching, she now works as a freelance writer and training consultant specializing in stress-related matters and interpersonal communication. She lives in Guildford, Surrey with her partner.

D0289340

Overcoming Common Problems

THE GOOD STRESS GUIDE

Mary Hartley

First published in Great Britain in 1995 by
Sheldon Press, SPCK, Marylebone Road, London NW1 4DU

British Library Cataloguing-in-Publication Data
A catalogue record for this book is available from the British Library

ISBN 0–85969–712–6

Photoset by Deltatype Ltd, Ellesmere Port, Cheshire
Printed in Great Britain by Biddles Ltd, Guildford and King's Lynn

Contents

1

What is stress?

Exploring perceptions

The word 'stress' is very powerful and emotive. It has a multitude of meanings and associations, depending on who is using it. Often the word seems to capture a feeling of high-powered life in the fast lane, a life of pressures and demands that is the price one has to pay for living in the late twentieth century. It is also a word that is used for the overstretched parent and the overpressurized executive, the student facing exams and the celebrity coping with fame. We associate it with harmful and negative events and see it as something to be avoided. In engineering, poetry or music, however, 'stress' is natural and desirable, not destructive and harmful.

The following three exercises will help you to focus on your own ideas and preconceptions regarding stress.

Exercise 1

Jot down all the words, ideas and associations that come to mind when you hear the word 'stress'. Circle any words you feel are particularly significant to you.

Exercise 2

Read the following check-list and tick each statement according to whether you believe it to be true or false, then write what you believe stress to be at the end.

1

	True	False
Stress is an illness.	☐	☐
Stress is always bad for you.	☐	☐
Stress is caused by other people doing things to you.	☐	☐
Stress is something that happens in your mind.	☐	☐
Stress can be measured in your body.	☐	☐
Stress is best treated by tranquillizers.	☐	☐
Stress attacks inadequate people.	☐	☐
Stress is inevitable in this day and age.	☐	☐
Stress is something to hide from others.	☐	☐
Stress is something to hide from yourself.	☐	☐

Stress is : ....

Exercise 3

Complete the following statements as often as you wish:

I feel stressed when: ....

I feel stressed when: ....

I feel stressed when: ....

These exercises will have helped you to focus on your ideas about stress and to identify areas of your life that you associate with stressful feelings. As you work through the book, you will probably find you want to add to some of your original responses, making changes in the light of further exploration of the subject and your own experiences.

Defining stress

The following study sheet offers some ideas about stress that will enable you to think more helpfully about your experience and perception of it.

Study sheet 1

Your responses to the previous exercises probably show that, like most of us, you associate stress with unpleasant and unwelcome experiences, in spite of all the variety of definitions there are of this word.

However, stress is not, in itself, destructive. Pressure, in itself, does not constitute stress. Stress is generated by your *response* to an inappropriate level of pressure. 'Inappropriate' does not necessarily mean 'excessive'.

Believe it or not, too *little* pressure can be as much a source of stress as too much. Too little stimulus can lead to apathy and boredom. Some pressure is actually good for us. The ideal situation occurs when we can respond in a stimulated and alert way to pressure and demands. The point at which this happens is a very fine one. Once the demand moves above or below the appropriate level for you, the balance begins to tip. This is when we experience what we call 'stress' — when there is tension between the pressure that is placed on us and our ability to cope with it. So stress is not, in itself, destructive. In fact, it is essential.

Hans Selye, the doctor who conducted early research into the effects of stress on the body, says: 'Complete freedom from stress is death because all human activity involves stress.'[1]

Selye describes the pleasurable feeling that we experience when we are equal to and enjoy the pressure put on us as 'eustress'. This is the buzz we get when the balance is right. It's a question of judging when the balance is right for you. When the balance is right we experience the kind of energy and dynamism that makes stress not only an essential but a positive experience. We can learn to use our personal and physical resources to meet the challenge of stress and channel it so that it becomes a motivating force that can lead to greater self-awareness and self-confidence and help us to lead more rewarding lives.

Stress is subjective. It is not physically 'out there', waiting to attack. Stress is the result of an individual's response to a situation. It can be managed and its harmful effects reduced, so that it works for us and not against us.

Responses to pressure

When we are feeling under pressure, our whole system responds to the situation and any part of our system can show a reaction. Each of us has a unique response, depending on our own individual make-up.

All our responses can be divided among the four main areas of human functioning:

- emotional
- mental
- behavioural
- physical.

The scenario below and the exercise that follows illustrate these and will help you begin to identify the ways in which different parts of our system can react when we are under pressure.

Scenario 1

Thank God for 'Neighbours', thought Cathy as she put the children's tea in front of them. Half an hour's peace and quiet. Her head had been throbbing persistently all morning.

She had thought she had been hiding it well by pretending to be immersed in her work, but when Helen Johnson looked at her sympathetically and said, 'You look awful. Why don't you go home?' she had almost burst into tears.

It was all very well to say, 'Why don't you go home?', but only the other morning Derek Hall had made a snide comment about women who have a few days off every month. He looked very startled when she snapped at him. She hadn't meant to, it just slipped out.

She really ought to pay those bills she'd left out on the dining-room table, but there was a load to put in the washing machine first, not to mention a huge pile of ironing sitting there reproachfully. The whole point of her working only part-time was so that she would have time to do all the other things on her plate but, somehow, the hours just drifted away.

She sat down and opened the chequebook determinedly. Probably a cup of tea and a biscuit would make her feel better and help her to concentrate. She got up and switched on the kettle. About 20 minutes later, she was staring at two completed bills and an empty packet of chocolate biscuits she could hardly remember eating.

'Neighbours' over, the children had started squabbling noisily. She wondered if she could summon up the energy to put them to bed. The front door opened and Trevor came in whistling noisily. She winced. 'Must you make such a row? I've got a splitting headache.'

'What, again? I don't know what's wrong with you these days. You'd better snap out of it soon, we're meeting Richard and Penny in two hours.' She looked at him blankly. 'Don't say you've forgotten?'

'It went straight out of my head. I've had so much to do. . . . I haven't got a babysitter or anything. . . .'

'Oh, that's great!' The door slammed behind him.

Never mind, she thought. It would be quite a relief not to go out. She might get that ironing done.

Trevor felt buzzing with energy as he drove to the office. He had spent most of the previous evening working on the figures for next week's meeting and intended putting them on everyone's desk before they arrived. Just as well, really, that they'd had to put Richard and Penny off. He didn't enjoy seeing them much these days in any case. They didn't seem to have much in common any more and they never really seemed to understand when he talked about his problems at work.

He liked the early morning, when the place was still empty. No problem getting in good and early, either, as he was usually awake and raring to go at 5.40 a.m. no matter how late he got to bed. He kept a notebook on the bedside table to jot down things that occurred to him during the night or when he woke up.

No need to waste time on breakfast, either. He just ignored Cathy's nagging and told her he would get something as soon as the canteen opened. The truth was that he didn't feel like eating that much these days. His stomach seemed to get upset very easily. Still, it's healthier not to eat too much, and who has time for a 'proper lunch' anyway? He counted himself lucky he could keep going on tea and cigarettes — rather more cigarettes than he'd like, but there you are.

He picked up his briefcase from the back seat of the car and strode purposefully to his office, giving a cheery 'Good morning' to Val Henderson as he passed her. Another one who liked an early start, obviously.

There was a note on his desk. Angela must have left it last night. It read, 'Trevor, sorry, but I've strained my back. Won't be in tomorrow.'

Damn and blast the woman! How was he supposed to operate without a secretary? Strained back, indeed. Just an excuse for skiving. He couldn't remember when he'd last had a day off for illness. He looked down in surprise at the pencil he had snapped off in his hand.

Val Henderson gazed at Trevor's retreating back. What on earth was wrong with him these days, she thought, walking everywhere with that funny, jerky stride as if there was a fire he had to put out. And the way he said, 'Good morning', so loudly, and as if his teeth were clenched. He should learn to take it easy, she thought.

She went into the kitchen area and put on the kettle. A cup of coffee, then she would find the notes she needed for this morning's interviews. Actually, though, she ought to get those memos out before this afternoon's meeting.

Waiting for the kettle to boil, she began to study the notices on the pinboard and become engrossed in a circular about pay-advice slips, then moved on to read the 'For Sale' cards. Remarkably good value, that mountain bike. Perhaps she should take it up. She drank her coffee thirstily. It had been a good evening, but it's true what they say about alcohol being dehydrating. She'd had a mouth like a tinderbox when she woke up — at the crack of dawn, too. Still, a small price to pay for

5

really relaxing and forgetting about work. It was a ritual she looked forward to, the first drink — usually Martini and lemonade or a white wine spritzer at about 6.30. She usually just had one or two, but last night had been a celebration.

She drained the cup and glanced at her watch. Oh, no, only a few minutes until the first interview. She'd have to get those notes and do the memos later. But there would be trouble if she didn't manage to get them done. She stood in the middle of the room, undecided.

Trevor walked by, muttering grimly, 'See Angela's off again?' She wished *she* was.

Exercise 4

Can you recognize any warning signs in the ways that Cathy, Trevor and Val are responding to their situations? Think about how their bodies are reacting, how they are feeling, how their thought patterns and concentration are affected, how their behaviour is affected. Jot down your findings under the following headings which, as we have seen, are the four main areas of human functioning.

	Physical	*Emotional*	*Mental*	*Behavioural*
Cathy	....			
Trevor	....			
Val	....			

How do you react under pressure?

Exercise 5

Read the check-lists below and tick the statements that apply to you.

The important thing here is to look for significant changes in the way you respond. Often, a change in pressure level will result in a change in your pattern of behaviour — but remember, it could be a change observed by others and not noticed by yourself. For this reason, it might be a good idea to discuss some of the questions on the check-lists with someone close

6

to you. There may be a trusted colleague who could give you useful information about your observable behaviour at work, and a friend or partner could do the same for your behaviour in other contexts.

Remember that the incidence of these effects will vary from individual to individual, as will their significance. Physical signs described here may have a physiological explanation unconnected with stress or pressure but, on the other hand, it is very easy to ignore these signs or attribute them too readily to other causes.

We all have our weak spots and become used to them — you might often have headaches or have 'always' suffered from poor digestion. It is important not to accept these symptoms as inevitable and very important not to explain them away. This point is re-emphasized in following sections.

Treat these check-lists, then, as a guide and a prompt. They may help you to identify a pattern of response. If you become aware of this you are more likely to be able to replace unthinking reflexes with different responses.

Check-list: behavioural changes

	Never	*Often*	*Frequently*
Do you notice an increase in alcohol consumption?	☐	☐	☐
Do you eat more than usual?	☐	☐	☐
Do you throw yourself into pointless activity?	☐	☐	☐
Are you unable to summon up energy?	☐	☐	☐
Do you find it hard to get to sleep?	☐	☐	☐
Do you smoke more than usual?	☐	☐	☐
Do you see less of people outside work?	☐	☐	☐
Do you take part in fewer activities not to do with work?	☐	☐	☐
Do you withdraw from contact with colleagues?	☐	☐	☐
Do you take time off work?	☐	☐	☐

Do you take sleeping tablets or tranquillizers?	☐	☐	☐
Do you get angry or irritated at home?	☐	☐	☐
Do you talk about work at home or with friends?	☐	☐	☐
Do you speak more loudly than usual?	☐	☐	☐
Do you speak more quietly than usual?	☐	☐	☐
Do you overreact to little things?	☐	☐	☐
Do you find it hard to finish when you start?	☐	☐	☐

Other ....

Check-list: physical changes

	Never	Often	Frequently
Do you suffer from headaches?	☐	☐	☐
Do you suffer from skin rashes?	☐	☐	☐
Do you get back pains?	☐	☐	☐
Do you get pains in the chest?	☐	☐	☐
Do you experience palpitations?	☐	☐	☐
Do you suffer from indigestion?	☐	☐	☐
Do your muscles feel stiff and tense?	☐	☐	☐
Do you feel that you may pass out?	☐	☐	☐
Do you get stomach pains or diarrhoea?	☐	☐	☐
Do you pick up any bug that's going around?	☐	☐	☐

Other ....

Check-list: emotional/mental changes

	Never	Often	Frequently
Do you worry for no particular reason?	☐	☐	☐
Do you keep forgetting things?	☐	☐	☐
Do you see yourself as a failure?	☐	☐	☐
Do you find it difficult to concentrate?	☐	☐	☐
Do you have panic attacks?	☐	☐	☐
Do you feel elated for no reason?	☐	☐	☐
Do you still enjoy the things you used to?	☐	☐	☐
Do you look forward to things?	☐	☐	☐
Do you feel restless all the time?	☐	☐	☐
Do you feel wound up?	☐	☐	☐
Do you find it hard to make decisions?	☐	☐	☐

Other ....

Fight or flight

Understanding how the body works when reacting to pressure is an important step towards managing stress. Although it is very difficult to do anything about our automatic responses, we can learn to give our bodies different messages about events so that the automatic reaction isn't so readily or so powerfully triggered.

Exercise 6

Turn back to Exercise 3 (page 2). Take the first situation identified on your list. Imagine yourself in this situation. What happens to you physically? Does your heart beat more quickly? Do you tense your muscles? Feel sick?

Working through your list of situations, jot down a brief description of how your body responds to each one.

My physical response is ....

My physical response is ....

My physical response is ....

Study sheet 2

Our bodies are programmed to deal with threat. Without the ability to stand up to danger, the human race would never have survived. When faced with danger, the body springs into action and prepares us for fight or flight. The preparation begins in the brain, the hypothalamus — this is the control centre. Its role is to interpret perception through experience and to send appropriate messages through the system. When it gets the message 'danger!', it relays it to the pituitary gland. This sends hormones on to the adrenal glands. Adrenalin is pumped out. Energy is mobilized. Your heart rate increases. Your breathing becomes rapid and your muscles tense. Your blood pressure rises. Blood rushes from the heart to the limbs in readiness for the exertion of greater muscular effort. Your saliva dries up. Your digestive system closes down. Your liver goes into action and produces more glucose for fuel. Your pupils dilate, your senses are alerted. You are ready to fight your opponent, or run for your life! Your body has adapted to the dangerous situation and you are in the first stage of what Hans Selye termed the 'general adaptation syndrome'.

The second stage is when the body tries to return to a state of equilibrium. Once action is taken, your body calms down. Another system comes into play. Your pancreas produces more insulin to bring down the levels of glucose in the blood. Your heart rate drops. Hormones are neutralized in the liver and digestion is resumed. Lactic acid created as a result of the muscular exertion is neutralized.

So, we have a store of adaptive energy that is triggered very quickly to enable us to cope with 'life or death' threats. Once the threat has been dealt with, arousal should return to its previous level. It doesn't always happen like that, however. Often, we are unable to fight or run away from our 'stressors'. We are also likely to encounter another stressor before we have had time to go through the second stage, so we remain in a state of arousal.

If you are constantly in a state of preparation for 'fight or flight', the very physiological changes designed to get you out of danger become dangerous. A permanently increased heart rate can lead to high blood pressure. Rapid breathing can lead to hyperventilation. Muscles tensed for exertion can cause aches and pains. Dilated pupils can lead to blurred vision. Glucose production can lead to excess sugar in the blood. The shutdown of the digestive system can lead to various digestive disorders. Sweating can affect the skin's surface and lead to rashes and skin diseases. And, if the balance isn't restored, your supply of adaptive energy is exhausted and you could pay the price in exhaustion or burn-out — the final stage.

It is important, therefore, to understand *how* you are using your energy when you respond to stress, how your behaviour changes from the way you function when the pressure level is right for you. Raised blood pressure and the inability to concentrate are not in themselves warning signs — some people experience these conditions all the time — and you won't necessarily exhibit all these symptoms if you are under stress anyway. Many people develop problems in one or two areas, their own particular weak spots. It is important not just to accept these symptoms as being inevitable, and very important not to explain them away. It is possible that your back pain *is* caused by carrying heavy piles of books or bags of shopping, but it could *also* be caused by mental stress. Hans Selye said, 'Stress becomes dangerous when it is unusually prolonged, comes too often or concentrates on one particular organ of the body.'[2]

The effects of stress on the body and the dangers of prolonged stress are far-reaching and incalculable. Stress-induced ailments include heart disease, high blood pressure, ulcers, headaches, disorders of the muscles and joints, respiratory and digestive problems and skin problems. It is widely accepted in medical circles that stress is a contributory factor in many cases of cancer. It is not the accumulation of stressful experiences themselves that can trigger these types of illness, but the fact that the immune system has been weakened by consistent exposure to harmful stress.

However, we can learn to discover the sources of our stress and to control them. We can strengthen our immune system and alleviate some of the symptoms presented by using the kind of stress management techniques described later in this book.

Exercise 7

Now look at the physical signs you described in the previous exercise and, referring to Study sheet 2, try to trace their likely physiological origin.

Achieving the right balance

You will now be aware of the very individual nature of the stress response and of the importance of identifying what is the *right* amount of pressure for you. The challenge is to identify and maintain the level of pressure that enables you to function effectively and consistently.

Remember, too little pressure can be as dangerous as too much, and the dividing line separating the manageable amount from the unmanageable is delicate and precarious.

We often speak of 'the last straw'. *Your* last straw could be anything from a minor change to a major crisis, but it's enough to make you topple from feeling confident and capable to feeling overwhelmed and unable to cope.

Pressure and demands do not, in themselves, constitute stress. Stress is the adaptive response of the body to any demand made on it and the demand may be unwelcome or pleasurable. The stress reactions of the body don't vary according to the nature of the 'stressor': a visit to the dentist's chair and an erotic kiss trigger the same physical responses of raised heartbeat and fast pulse!

Sometimes, we actively *seek* stressful situations, deliberately wanting a thrill. Think of fairground rides or driving fast or taking part in dangerous sports.

Sometimes, too, we leave things until the last minute or find other ways of making routine activities a little bit demanding to enhance our feeling of pleasure when they have been achieved.

Of course, our perception of what is demanding is different for each of us, and so is the way we respond. One person's threat is another person's challenge. Stress arises from the tension between the pressure placed on a person and the individual's ability to cope with it.

The next exercise will enable you to identify what is the right amount of pressure for you, focusing on what it is like for you when the pressure level is wrong, and what it feels like when you experience your optimum pressure level.

Exercise 8

Think of a time when you were under very *little* pressure, when you faced few demands or challenges. Concentrate for a few minutes on what it felt like to be you at that time. Jot down your observations under the following headings.

Emotional (How did you feel?)

....

....

....

....

Mental (How was your ability to think and concentrate affected?)

....

....

Behavioural (What changes occurred in the way you behaved?)

....

....

....

Physical (What happened to your body?)

....

....

....

Now think of a time when you were under a *lot* of pressure, when you faced heavy demands. Concentrate for a few minutes on what it felt like to be you at that time. Jot down your observations under the following headings.

Emotional (How did you feel?)

....

....

....

Mental (How was your ability to think and concentrate affected?)

....

....

....

Behavioural (What changes occurred in the way you behaved?)

....

....

....

Physical (What happened to your body?)

....

....

....

Now think of a time when the pressure level seemed *right* for you, when you enjoyed the demands made on you and felt you were functioning at your best. Concentrate for a few minutes on what it felt like to be you at that time. Jot down your observations under the following headings.

Emotional (How did you feel?)

....

....

....

Mental (How was your ability to think and concentrate affected?)

....

....

....

Behavioural (What changes occurred in the way you behaved?)

....

....

Physical (What happened to your body?)

....

....

....

Exercise 9

You should now have a picture of your particular patterns of response as
pressure levels change.

Concentrate on the *last* picture of yourself — when you were operating
under optimum pressure for you, when you were experiencing the
confidence and vitality associated with positive pressure.

Complete the following sentence as many times as you like, covering,
where appropriate, the four main areas — emotional, mental, behavioural, physical.

When the balance is right for me, I: ....

....

....

This is the ideal state, and it *can* be achieved. Stress can be managed and
controlled, and made to work for you.

2

Are you stress-prone?

Life events

You will realize by now that *any* event — no matter how insignificant it may seem to someone else — *can* act as a stressor. This is because any form of change is potentially stressful since change requires adaptation. It doesn't necessarily have to be an unwelcome or harmful demand. Change, in itself — whether a pleasant one like getting married or an unwelcome one like losing your job — imposes demands to which our bodies react with the stress response. Of course, the more critical the change, the greater the effort expended in adapting to it. During periods of change, therefore, our natural resistance to injury and disease is lowered. If this goes on for too long, there is greater danger of our succumbing to illness. Being aware of this, however, will enable us to be prepared for a period of challenge, and to strengthen our resources to meet its demands.

The level of pressure you are experiencing at the time of the change will influence your reaction to it. If you are already under a lot of pressure, a slight change in your circumstances can tip the balance, and you could find yourself experiencing illness or exhaustion. But, if you are below your optimum level of pressure, then you may view the same event as stimulating and challenging.

Exercise 10

Jot down below some of the changes that have occurred in your life recently. Don't just concentrate on major events, but think also about changes in routine at home or at work, and other alterations to your usual pattern of daily living.

Try to identify the level of pressure you were experiencing at the time, and how you reacted to the event.

Event	*Level of pressure*			*Response*
	High	Optimum	Low	
1	☐	☐	☐	
2	☐	☐	☐	

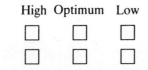

	High	Optimum	Low
3	☐	☐	☐
4	☐	☐	☐

You may have noticed that you coped well with major unwelcome changes, but surprisingly badly with minor events. This is partly to do with your mental and physical state at the time, but also the amount of change you experience in a short space of time. Major life crises face us all at some time, but less obvious sources of potential stress can have a cumulative effect. The greater the frequency of stressful events, the higher is the probability that you will develop stress-related symptoms.

Study sheet 3

The 'life event rating scale' was developed by medical researchers Thomas Holme and Richard Rahe. They studied more than 5000 people to see if there was a pattern of response to specific life events, ranging in severity from major ones, such as the death of a spouse, to trivial ones, such as getting a parking ticket. They listed 41 positive and negative events, and gave each one a score according to the amount of adjustment needed to come to terms with it. For each individual in the survey, they marked the event that had taken place within a certain period of time and added up the numbers. They found that people with high scores, who had experienced a cluster of life changes in a short space of time, were more likely to suffer a stress-related illness in the following two-year period.

The Holme Rahe scale

Life event	Life change units
Death of a spouse.	100
Divorce.	73
Marital relationship separation.	65
Imprisonment.	63
Death of a close family member.	63
Personal injury or illness.	53
Marriage.	50
Dismissal from work.	47
Retirement.	44
Change in health of family member.	40
Pregnancy.	39
Sexual difficulties.	39

Gaining a new family member.	39
Business readjustment.	39
Change in financial state.	38
Death of a close friend.	37
Change in number of arguments with spouse.	35
Change to a different line of work.	34
Major mortgage.	32
Son or daughter leaving home.	29
Trouble with in-laws.	29
Outstanding personal achievement.	28
Spouse begins or stops work.	26
Change in living conditions.	25
Revision of personal habits.	23
Trouble with the boss.	22
Change in recreational activities.	21
Change in social activities.	20
Change of schools.	20
Change in number of family reunions.	15
Holiday.	13
Christmas.	12
Minor violation of the law.	11

Exercise 11

You may find it helpful to apply Holme's and Rahe's findings to your own experience. Check off each event that has happened to you during the previous year. Total up your score.

A score of over 300 points in one year greatly increases your risk of suffering a stress-related health problem. A score of below 150 means you have experienced a relatively low amount of life change and that there is less likelihood of you experiencing harmful stress.

The results of this exercise may look alarming! But, remember, illness is not an *inevitable* result of change. You can adapt a change in such a way that you transform a potential hazard into an opportunity for growth and understanding of yourself and those around you. Change tests your tolerance level and your ability to adapt and regain balance. As we have seen, healthy tension is necessary to life. Responding positively to pressure enables you to achieve the balanced state you described in Exercise 7.

Understanding yourself and your reactions and being able to anticipate stressful periods is an important step in learning how to make stress work for you.

Your personality type

Scenario 2

Richard's fingers drummed impatiently on the steering wheel. That stupid person in front, holding everyone up. Now they'd missed the lights again — and that Renault alongside him looked as if it was going to cut in. He revved up warningly and shot away the second the lights changed, with a triumphant look at the driver.

In spite of the delay, Richard was in the office as usual on the dot of eight. He wrote memos to various colleagues while he read the Chairman's report, pausing only to highlight certain sections. When he'd finished the last memo, he dashed off to deliver them himself — no point in waiting until Jackie came in, it took her so long to do anything. It was always the same; the only way to get things done quickly and properly was to do them yourself. He jabbed the lift button a few times and, irritated by its slowness, ran up the stairs to the Marketing Department. It had been a good meeting yesterday, but he'd had to keep making people get to the point. Perhaps they resented him for behaving like that, but it was certainly effective, and got the results Head Office wanted.

Penny looked up and smiled as he strode in. 'Morning, Richard. Cup of coffee?' Richard frowned. 'No time. Can you read this, Penny — it's something arising from yesterday's meeting.'

Penny took the memo and put it on her desk. 'OK. I'll read it later.'

'Actually, I'd like your response as soon as possible — about five minutes ago, in fact!', Richard half-joked.

'Well, I'm in the middle of this mailshot. I'll deal with your paper when I've finished it.'

She watched Richard dash off to Charlie's desk. It must be very wearing to be him, she thought. Take that meeting. He couldn't let anyone finish what they were saying, just had to interrupt with his own ideas. And you could see him switching off when Charlie brought up the Hadley account, just because it wasn't his particular area of interest. Then, asking him to hurry up like that! Penny shook her head ruefully and worked slowly and methodically through her task. She would never be singled out for the fast track like Richard, but she enjoyed her work and expected to get where she wanted in her own time.

She looked forward to a good long coffee break after finishing this and before reading Richard's memo.

Exercise 12

You may recognize elements of your own behaviour and personality in the descriptions of Richard and Penny. Think about the way you feel and behave, then answer the following questions.

	Yes	No
Do you usually do several things at once?	☐	☐
Are you very competitive?	☐	☐
Do you dislike or feel guilty about relaxing?	☐	☐
Are you bored when other people are talking?	☐	☐
Do you interrupt people?	☐	☐
Are you always in a hurry?	☐	☐
Do you find it hard to wait patiently?	☐	☐
Do you tend to hide your feelings?	☐	☐
Do you speak emphatically and forcefully?	☐	☐
Do you find it hard to delegate?	☐	☐
Do you do things (e.g. eating, walking) quickly?	☐	☐
Are you irritated with people who dawdle?	☐	☐
Are you physically tense?	☐	☐
Do you find it difficult to relate to other people's interests?	☐	☐
Do you have few interests outside work?	☐	☐
Do you find it hard to take things one at a time?	☐	☐

If you answered 'Yes' to all these questions, you are what has been described as a 'Type A' personality. The number of affirmative answers you ticked indicates how strong is your tendency towards this type of behaviour. If you answered 'No' to all or many of the questions, you are the opposite type of personality — 'Type B'. Is either personality type particularly prone to stress? Although we are all potentially stress-prone, research has shown that Type As are more susceptible to stress-related illnesses because of particular aspects of character and particular mental attitudes.

Study sheet 4

Type A and Type B patterns of behaviour are terms that were first coined by Meyer Friedman and Dr Ray Rosenman, two heart specialists who conducted an eight-year study into the effects of stress on the heart.[3] They identified alternative patterns of behaviour that they categorized as A or B.

Type A individuals are competitive and hard-driving. They are impatient with themselves and with others, and are inflexible in their approach. They are generally aggressive achievers who set themselves unrealistic deadlines and push themselves hard. Often described as workaholics, they like deadlines and pressure, and are intolerant of weakness in themselves or others. This type of person likes to feel in control and can be driven to distraction by waiting in queues and traffic jams. Often only a slight provocation can trigger angry and hostile outbursts. They engage in multiple behaviour, doing several things at once, often at inappropriate times. Type As may deliberately seek out the kind of change that will impose great demands on their mind and body.

Type B individuals take life more calmly. They maintain realistic deadlines and do not value work as highly as Type As. They are less impatient and tend to work more slowly and methodically. They know how to relax and can separate work and leisure. They can tolerate delays and can be calm and patient with people and events.

Friedman and Rosenman found that Type A people are between two and three times more likely to have a stroke or heart attack than Type B people, even if they are doing the same sort of work and living in the same conditions. They have a greater cardiovascular response to stress and their system is almost permanently mobilized for action, usually ready for fight rather than flight. When given a mental arithmetic task to complete, Type As and Type Bs performed equally well, but Type As responded to the task as if responding to a crisis. They released 40 times the amount of stress hormones into their bloodstream, 3 times the amount of blood flowing to their muscles, and sent 4 times as much adrenalin surging through their blood vessels than did the Type Bs. All their stress responses were activated, and they were in the state of arousal that is the habitual, and dangerous, condition many Type A individuals exhibit.

Since this original research, other research has been carried out, most of which confirms Friedman and Rosenman's findings, that behavioural patterns and physical disorders are closely related. However, this is not to say that Type A behaviour will *inevitably* end in illness or that it is totally dangerous and undesirable. Many satisfied and successful people show classic Type A behaviour. Indeed, the kind of drive and ambition exhibited by those in this category is welcomed and encouraged in competitive environments. Also, many of us may have some Type A characteristics *and* some Type B, although usually one category will predominate. A perfect balance of both behaviours is very rare and is probably an unrealistic ideal. Behaviour patterns that *can* be achieved are those that harness and channel the *positive* aspects of Type A behaviour so that pressure becomes a stimulating challenge rather than a harmful stimulus.

Of course, Type As have to *want* to change. They have to be convinced that some modification of their behaviour is essential if they are to avoid stress-related illnesses. One way of encouraging Type As to value Type B characteristics is to present them with some of the harmful results of stress they are likely to encounter — results that may well prevent them from performing effectively the activities which give them so much pleasure and fulfilment.

In Chapter 1, we looked at the physical, emotional, mental and behavioural changes brought about by stress. Type As are often told they are heading for a heart attack if they carry on as they are. A frequent response is to shrug off this warning or even to take some secret pride in it — such illnesses being regarded as badges of honour for those who live in the fast lane. Type As could consider more carefully the *other* effects of their overpressurized lifestyle, such as the *mental* effects of too much stress. They could find themselves unable to concentrate, liable to lose the thread of what they are saying in mid-sentence, unable to remember even familiar material. They are likely to make more mistakes and be unable to think or plan clearly. These consequences are alarming for ambitious, achievement-orientated Type As, and knowing about them may persuade them to channel their energy into achieving a goal of optimum mental and physical fitness that will enable them to continue to operate at a high level of achievement and activity. A good route to this is to monitor your behaviour and set yourself goals by which you can assess the success of your move towards different behaviour. You can use your Type A determination and drive to enable you to achieve goals and maintain energy and motivation the Type B way, which produces results *without* causing physical and mental damage.

Type A behaviour *can* be managed. We can learn to modify the way we act and consciously adopt Type B characteristics, enabling us to do all the things Type As do but without their usual harmful effects. With practice and conscious effort, unhelpful Type A habits can be replaced with new Type B behaviour.

Exercise 13

Think of ways in which you can introduce Type B behaviour into your life. Identify specific situations and ways in which you could react and behave differently. The first situation is presented as an example, but think of as many others as you can, then list the circumstances and the changes you will introduce. Also, decide when you will begin to put these changes into effect.

Situation	Type A behaviour	Possible change
Eating	Rapid, perhaps doing something else at same time.	Put down knife and fork between each bite. Chew each mouthful slowly.

Exercise 14

Work out a system of penalizing yourself for unhelpful Type A behaviour. For example, if you overtake a car for no reason other than impatience and a sense of being in a hurry, slow down and let two cars overtake *you*. If you interrupt someone who is speaking to you, make yourself listen for a certain length of time before making a contribution to the conversation. Look at your own behaviour and write down examples that are relevant to you below.

Behaviour	Penalty	Reward

Now choose a reward for completing the penalty! Decide what kind of treat will be enjoyable and appropriate. Make it recreational and not job-related. It could be something like buying yourself a small indulgent item or having a leisurely cup of coffee or enjoying a long soak in a bubble bath.

Exercise 15

Use the powerful method of self-instruction to work yourself into less hurried behaviour and to reduce your Type A urgency about time. Remind yourself to do things quietly and calmly. Use sentences like, 'I don't need to hurry. There is no need to hurry. I know what I am doing and I need not hurry. Nothing bad will happen if I don't hurry.' Devise the kind of self-talk that will work for you and practise saying it slowly and rhythmically until you can automatically call on it when you find yourself falling into Type A behaviour, such as doing several things at once or speaking quickly and sharply.

In the following chapters and later on in the book, you will find more suggestions and exercises you can use to help you change your behaviour and attitudes. You will see how you can use your mind and your imagination to achieve the goals you have set yourself, how to visualize yourself acting in the desired way until the imagination becomes fact. In the last chapter you will find suggestions for relaxation, which Type As should find particularly helpful!

Scenario 3

Julia looked at her watch with irritation as Karen waltzed into the office. Karen intercepted her glance.

'I'm only a *bit* late', she said cheerfully. 'I've been up for ages, actually, but I couldn't decide what to wear!' She poured herself a cup of coffee and put it on her desk, slopping some of it over the side.

Julia winced and tried to concentrate on the report she was reading. She just didn't understand Karen. Admittedly she was bright and good at her job, but she was so casual about timekeeping. Julia prided herself on never being late; she would rather arrive anywhere half an hour early than be a minute late. It was true that Jenny, her boss, was quite relaxed about such matters as long as the job got done, but Julia set herself certain standards and wasn't going to let them slip. She didn't understand this business of not knowing what to wear, either. She had her outfits for the week ready every Sunday evening, with shoes and bags precisely lined up. She would actually find it quite difficult to get to sleep if she hadn't.

'Do you want a drink?', asked Karen.

Automatically Julia checked her watch again. She always had a cup of tea and two bourbon biscuits at half past ten. She said, 'No thanks', and tried not to look at the piles of paper covering Karen's desk. Her own desk was immaculately neat. This was another point of pride.

Jenny poked her head round the door. 'What do you think of those recommendations, Julia? I like the one about reorganizing the ordering system. It will be chaos at first, but we'll benefit in the long run.'

Julia hated the thought of changing the system she had been used to for so long. She felt little flutters of panic in her stomach and straightened the already straight row of pencils on her desk.

Exercise 16

You may recognize parts of Julia's behaviour and reactions. Think about the way you feel and behave, and answer the following questions to help you to identify any similar aspects in your own behaviour.

On a scale of one to ten, where one is the lowest and ten the highest, tick the number that reflects how strongly you agree or disagree with the statement.

	1	2	3	4	5	6	7	8	9	10
I pride myself on my competence.	☐	☐	☐	☐	☐	☐	☐	☐	☐	☐
I like things ordered and predictable.	☐	☐	☐	☐	☐	☐	☐	☐	☐	☐
I enjoy detail.	☐	☐	☐	☐	☐	☐	☐	☐	☐	☐
I like the little rituals of work and home life.	☐	☐	☐	☐	☐	☐	☐	☐	☐	☐
I dislike any change.	☐	☐	☐	☐	☐	☐	☐	☐		☐
I dislike muddle.	☐	☐	☐	☐	☐	☐	☐	☐	☐	☐
I don't understand people who tolerate mess and muddle.	☐	☐	☐	☐	☐	☐	☐	☐	☐	☐
I like things cut and dried.	☐	☐	☐	☐	☐	☐	☐	☐	☐	☐

If you strongly agree with several of these statements it is probable that you, like Julia, are an obsessional type. You like things to be stable and predictable and actually take a pride in your insistence on neatness and order. You like things done in a certain way, and may find you become quite agitated if your rituals and routines are disturbed. This means that you are probably strongly resistant to change and new challenges, and your inflexibility may well lead you to develop various stress-related ailments.

However, this type of behaviour can also be modified and managed, so that your industry, conscientiousness and competence become real strengths, increasing your effectiveness rather than threatening to hinder it. The first step is to recognize potential dangers in your behaviour and identify ways of changing it. The very act of completing this exercise is an important step on the road to greater flexibility.

Exercise 17

Using the list in the previous exercise as a base, rank below the attitudes and characteristics you have that put you in this category placing first the behaviour you are most keen on and so on, or any tendencies you have towards this kind of behaviour. Describe them in terms of your own behaviour — that is, in the next column give, say, three examples of some of your habits and patterns that result from your attitude. For example, you may hate mess or muddle and one of your behaviours that results could be that you can't concentrate on a discussion if it takes place at an untidy desk or you can't leave the house in the morning unless everything is perfectly in order.

Attitude   *Behaviour*

Now think carefully about the behaviours you have described and their effects. There may have been occasions when your behaviour was beneficial. For example, your desire for tidiness meant that you could find an important item very quickly. There may also have been occasions when you have functioned less effectively than you might have or felt yourself under a great deal of pressure *because* of your desire for order and predictability or because of any of the attitudes on your list.

Choose three of your strongest attitudes and consider the helpful and the unhelpful effects of the behaviour that results, writing your answer in the spaces below. Don't just think about the effects on you, but on others and on the wider circumstances.

Attitude	*Helpful effects*	*Unhelpful effects*

You should now be able to focus clearly on the strengths in your behaviour and on the potentially dangerous areas that could be creating too much pressure for you, either now or in the future. The following exercise will help you begin to change the unhelpful behaviour. One example is given to help you get started.

Exercise 18

Situation	*Obsessional behaviour*	*Possible change*
Tea break	Having it exactly at the same time every day.	Having it a little earlier or later.

Exercise 19

Think about ways (unconnected to your personality type) in which you can make your behaviour more flexible. Choose minor changes you can make to your way of life. Although they may have little direct bearing on the critical aspects of your behaviour, they will help you to become accustomed to the idea of change and make you more resilient to coping with the kind of change that is imposed on you and which you, in particular, find very hard to cope with. Think of as many as possible and determine to try one or two a week. The first two are examples of the sorts of things you could do.

Alter my route to work slightly.
Read a different newspaper for a week.

....

....

....

....

....

....

....

....

It is very likely that your personality traits are making your experience of life very narrow. Your desire to have things organized and clear-cut may mean that you have little tolerance for activities that are, by their nature, ambiguous and intangible. Paying some attention to the creative and imaginative side of experience will help you to see yourself and the world from a different perspective and develop a less closed and restricted viewpoint, thereby strengthening your personal resources and increasing your resistance to harmful stress.

Exercise 20

This is a simple exercise for exploring your personality creatively and presenting those characteristics you have just been considering, as well as other elements of your character, in an entirely different form.

It is important not to take more than three minutes for this exercise — do it without thinking too much.

Imagine yourself as a tree. Draw the tree here.

Now look at what you have drawn and write a description of it, using the first person — 'I'. In your description, expand on the drawing by making comments describing yourself in detail. For example, 'My trunk is long and slender and my roots are thin and delicate.'

Here are some points you might like to consider in your description.

Where am I situated?
What are my branches like?
What are my roots like?
Is anything (birds, animals, something unidentified) in my tree?
How tall am I?
Do I have leaves, fruit, berries?

What is the weather like?
What is the general impression I create?

Scenario 4

Andrew was shaking with rage as he walked into the staffroom. It was the third time running Brett Collins had failed to hand in his homework and he hadn't even had the respect to offer a decent excuse.

'Who on earth does he think he is?', he exclaimed. 'How *dare* he treat me like that!'

Sandy yawned. 'Don't take it so seriously, Andrew! Why let a little thing like that get to you?'

'It might be a little thing to you,' said Andrew, 'but I don't see it that way. You should have seen the insolent expression on his face! I'm going to take this further.'

'Calm down a bit', said Sandy. He liked Andrew; he was usually a pleasant colleague and was known to be a good teacher. If only he wasn't so touchy, so ready to get on his high horse if he thought his authority was being challenged. He pushed a card towards him.

'Sign this before you go — it's for Peter's retirement.'

'Oh yes.' As Andrew wrote a message wishing Peter good luck for the future, he suppressed a shiver at the thought that he too would be retiring soon. He hated the idea of no longer having his professional label and description as a way of presenting himself to the world.

He glanced out of the window and saw Brett Collins in the playground amusing a group of friends with what he was sure was an imitation of him in their confrontation. 'He's for the high jump now!'

'Don't you think you're overreacting just a little?', suggested Sandy. 'Sometimes it's better just to let things go.'

'Perhaps you don't value your professionalism as much as I do', said Andrew as he headed for the playground.

Sandy sighed and started to make up a little rhyme for Peter's card. Lucky Peter, he would now have time to garden and do more work for his church, which was something he'd wanted to do for ages. Teaching was just *part* of his life, not like poor old Andrew.

Exercise 21

Maybe some of your attitudes are similar to Andrew's. Think about yourself and your attitude to your job, and answer the following questions. On a scale of one to ten, where one is the lowest and ten the highest, tick the number that reflects how strongly you agree or disagree with the statement.

ARE YOU STRESS-PRONE?

	1	2	3	4	5	6	7	8	9	10
My job title is very important to me.	☐	☐	☐	☐	☐	☐	☐	☐	☐	☐
I feel threatened if my professional competence is challenged.	☐	☐	☐	☐	☐	☐	☐	☐	☐	☐
I see promotion as recognition of my personal worth.	☐	☐	☐	☐	☐	☐	☐	☐	☐	☐
I feel my job gives me standing in my own eyes.	☐	☐	☐	☐	☐	☐	☐	☐	☐	☐
I feel my job gives me standing in other people's eyes.	☐	☐	☐	☐	☐	☐	☐	☐	☐	☐
I dislike the idea of not being able to identify myself by my job.	☐	☐	☐	☐	☐	☐	☐	☐	☐	☐

If you strongly agree with several of these statements, it is probable that you, like Andrew, are an over-identifier. This means that you may be investing too much of yourself in your job. If you see yourself primarily in terms of your employment, you are very vulnerable to anything that threatens or challenges you in that capacity. One of the consequences is that you begin to lose a sense of proportion and may become very aggressive or defensive when you feel your professionalism is being undermined.

You can change your attitude to work by thinking more widely about your life and achieving a greater sense of balance and proportion so that the qualities that make you effective at work enhance your whole existence and become a benefit rather than a potential danger.

Exercise 22

Think about yourself not in terms of your job, but in terms of your life outside work — your family, friends, interests, personal qualities. Complete the following sentence as many times as you can (the first two have been completed as examples).

I am . . . Josh's mother/father.
I am . . . Simon's friend.

I am ....

Now, take each of your statements in turn and identify *one* activity that you could undertake in each of your different roles.

I am . . .	Josh's mother/father.
This week I will . . .	read to him at bedtime twice.
I am . . .	Simon's friend.
This week I will . . .	arrange to meet him for a drink.

I am ....

....

....

This week I will ....

....

....

Repeat the exercise as often as you like, changing 'week' to 'month'.

Then, repeat it again, changing 'month' to 'year'.

You should now have a full picture of yourself. You are a person who functions in many capacities other than as a worker and, by committing yourself to certain activities in the short and long term, you are beginning to redress the balance and finding more of yourself in areas outside your job.

Exercise 23

Think about the particular satisfactions and enjoyments you derive from your work. For example, being part of a team may be very important to you or being in a position of authority. You may value the fact that your work helps other people or you may like the opportunities it gives you to see projects through from beginning to end. Choose the five most important aspects and list them below.

1 ....

2 ....

3 ....

4 ....

5 ....

Now think if there are other ways of gaining these particular satisfactions or ones like them. For example, if you like being useful to other people, are there any opportunities outside work for helping others? If you particularly value the camaraderie of the workplace, are there other places (clubs or pubs, maybe) that may offer a similar kind of companionship? For each of the points you have just listed, think of ways in which you could find a similar kind of enjoyment and write them down below.

1 ....

2 ....

3 ....

4 ....

5 ....

By considering other outlets and other areas of satisfaction, you are moving towards a more balanced outlook and strengthening your ability to cope with change in your working life. You should now have some idea of the attitudes that are making you vulnerable to stress and be able to make specific preparations to equip yourself to meet potential threats — such as retirement, redundancy or enforced moves — with greater resilience and fortitude.

Study sheet 5

You now know that certain personality types are likely to experience stress-related symptoms if their behaviour isn't modified.

However, aspects of the behaviour and attitudes of these types are positive and valuable and may be channelled in such a way as to experience the good kind of stress — the balance of pressure and reaction — that is challenging and exhilarating. The competitive and goal-orientated Type A can learn to control and manage the drive that leads to success and satisfaction. The obsessional type can learn to adapt to his or her environment and to other people so that the desire for meticulousness and orderliness becomes an *aid* to a balanced perspective rather than a *barrier* to it. The over-identifier can benefit from their pride in their work rather than be consumed by it.

The exercises you have completed have indicated ways of developing healthy coping strategies, using your personal resources to help you modify your behaviour. Remember that the ability to handle pressure is a learned skill and you can learn different ways of dealing with demands so that panic behaviour can be kept for situations that really *are* crises. Using strategies to help you match the intensity of your reaction to the seriousness of the situation will lead to long-term positive effects. Some benefits you are likely to experience are increased confidence, improved health and the ability to harness the power and energy of stress to help you function more effectively and dynamically.

There is also a personality type that is characterized by a high stress tolerance level. There are three marked characteristics of this type: *control*, *commitment* and *a sense of purpose*. Stress-resistant people have a sense of control over situations and events. They believe that they can influence the course of events and they accept some responsibility for what happens to them rather than seeking to blame other people or fate for events in their lives. They also have a sense of commitment, of involvement in whatever they are doing. Their lives are marked by a sense of purpose and direction. Finally, they view change as challenge. They anticipate the disruption associated with it and view it as an opportunity rather than a threat.

Exercise 24

Try seeing yourself as this kind of stress-resistant personality. Use the following statements to help you feel what it's like. Don't wait until you are faced with pressure, but say them to yourself regularly, perhaps at the beginning of each day.

- When I'm committed to something, I feel involved and full of energy.
- I enjoy change — it's exciting and full of possibilities.
- I like taking control of situations.
- When I'm faced with a stressful situation, I can make it positive.
- Stress brings out my positive qualities.

'There is nothing either good or bad But thinking makes it so.' (Hamlet)

This section focuses on understanding that stress lies in the individual's perception of an event rather than necessarily in the event itself. Stress exists in the reaction of the person to the situation. It's all in the eye of the beholder and varies with every person. Of course, there are certain stressors that affect most people negatively, but even in these cases the amount of pressure experienced will vary from person to person, as will the total perception of the situation. Even negative events can be turned into positive experiences if we adjust the way we perceive them and the ways we act.

Scenario 5

Judy drew her chair closer to the couple opposite. 'It's a lovely idea, this welcome party for us', she said.

'Well, we're pleased the house next door has been bought at last. It will be good to have a family living there', said Nancy.

Judy looked round the groups of people chatting and serving themselves from the buffet. 'What kind of neighbourhood is this? What are the people like?'

Mark asked, 'What were the people like in your old neighbourhood?'

Judy wrinkled her nose in an expression of distaste. 'To tell you the truth, they were a bit nasty. Very gossipy and backbiting.'

'Well,' said Mark, 'I guess you'll find people round here much the same.'

He wandered off to the other side of the room where Harry was leaning against the mantelpiece. 'How's it going, Harry? Are you beginning to feel at home?'

'Just finding my feet, Mark. Tell me, what's it like round here? What are the neighbours like?'

Mark asked, 'What were they like where you came from?'

Harry smiled. 'Fine — very friendly, chatty and lively.'

'Well,' said Mark, 'I guess you'll find people round here the same.'

Study sheet 6

We each perceive the world and construct our own experiences of events differently. Even if two people observe the same situation at the same time, they are likely to notice different things and give different accounts of it. Perception is a process of selecting, organizing and interpreting information we take in through all our senses. The first stage in the process of perception is the selection of information. This is to do with what we actually see and what we actually see depends on a number of factors. Some of these factors are external and some are internal — to do with our own personalities. Our individual needs, motives and interests govern what we perceive. You may have noticed that if you're thinking of buying a certain make of car, for example, the roads suddenly seem full of that particular model. In fact, there is just the same number as there was before, but now you are aware of them. If you're out shopping and beginning to feel hungry, you notice restaurant signs and are aware of food smells that you hadn't noticed before. Many pregnant women suddenly find their world is full of other pregnant women. Again, this is because of their heightened awareness of pregnancy. We all tend to pay attention to what interests us, and often we see and hear what we *want* to see and hear.

Feeling nervous at night, we are conscious of every little noise, which reinforces our fear whereas in daylight the same noise would go unnoticed.

Once we have selected or chosen what we perceive, we organize this information and interpret it so that it makes sense and fits our view of the world. We are strongly guided in this by our past experiences and past learning. That is, the ideas about life we learned as children and the kind of education and training we have received will affect how we perceive people and events. For example, someone skilled in car mechanics will view a car engine very differently from someone with an untrained eye; someone with a keen interest in fashion will perceive what people are wearing very differently from someone who thinks the main purpose of clothes is to keep you warm and covered!

The whole process of perception is, of course, very rapid and unconscious. Often we are hardly aware that we are investing a person or a situation with the potential to act as a stressor. Alfred Adler said, 'We are not influenced by facts but by our interpretation of facts.' Adler was a contemporary of Sigmund Freud and his work on childhood feelings of inferiority and how they can be overcome presents an optimistic approach to life, based on goal-setting, self-evaluation and the possibility of change through active effort. 'The power of human beings to turn a minus into a plus is among the finest and noblest of all human characteristics.' Adler's words indicate that we can interrupt and change the direction of our thoughts by making deliberate attempts to turn the negative into the positive.

Exercise 25

Think of ways in which you can make potentially negative experiences positive ones. List five examples. The first has been filled in to give you an idea of the sorts of things you can do.

1	Being in a traffic jam.
I can . . .	listen to a tape.
I can . . .	plan what I will do when I get to my destination.
I can . . .	finish the crossword.

2 ....

I can . . . .

I can . . . .

I can . . . .

3 ....

I can . . . .

I can . . . .

I can . . . .

4 ....

I can . . . .

I can . . . .

I can . . . .

5 ....

I can . . . .

I can . . . .

I can . . . .

Taking these practical steps to turn negative experiences into positive ones is a major way in which we can condition ourselves to cope with stress. We can modify our behaviour and our attitudes so that we can turn harmful stress into positive stress. The combination of thought and behaviour is immensely powerful. We can use our thoughts to influence how we feel and we can condition ourselves to respond in helpful ways.

The following sections consider how our behaviour can be governed by deep-rooted and childhood beliefs and attitudes that can be changed, and should be changed, if they are the cause of harmful stress and pressure.

Messages from the past

The way we perceive events and situations is influenced a great deal by ideas we developed in childhood and the values and beliefs with which we grew up. The beliefs and ideas we learned then were essential for our survival; they helped us to make sense of the world and gave us a basis for forming opinions about our own and others' behaviour.

However, these beliefs may not still apply. We've forgotten forming them and we are not consciously aware of them, but they could be contributing to the pressure we feel. We could be burdening ourselves with the baggage of ideas about the world and people's behaviour that are inappropriate for our lives now and which actually limit our resources for coping with stress. If we are to develop different attitudes to stressful situations, it may be necessary to work on changing some of our past messages. This may not be easy. Our value systems are likely to be fixed, inflexible parts of our personalities, and our central beliefs, those at the very core of our being, will be very hard to shift. But they can be altered: they have been learned; they can be unlearned. By re-evaluating the way we look at the world, we can meet the challenge of stressful situations by responding and making decisions in ways that are in keeping with the people we are today. Examining and questioning our inherited beliefs will enable us to develop more positive, optimistic approaches and responses.

The first step is to recognize behaviour patterns and persistent attitudes that are unhelpful to our lives now.

Scenario 6

Vicky found that her hands were shaking as she gathered together her papers and kept her head lowered so that no one would see the blush she felt creeping over her face and neck. She was amazed to hear Ted and Tricia laughing together and agreeing that there was nothing they enjoyed so much as a good, lively meeting. 'A frank and open exchange of views', mocked Tricia, and Ted exploded into loud laughter as they re-enacted the heated discussion in which they had both played leading roles.

It was all right for them. They clearly found the loud and vehement discussion stimulating. She hated raised voices, always had. She couldn't bear to hear people shouting. She always felt as if they were shouting at her.

In fact, she'd had several very relevant points she'd wanted to contribute, but she had shrunk from speaking out. Her mouth went dry when she heard raised voices and saw aggressive gesticulations. She actually found herself flinching and wishing she could sink into the ground. Now, as Ted, Tricia and the others moved towards the door, she mentally kicked herself. Once again she'd sat through the meeting without making a contribution. She knew she had helped to consolidate the others' idea of her as an ineffectual and uninvolved member of the team. This reflection made her feel worse and she realized that she dreaded the next meeting.

Vicky's reaction to loud voices and forceful gestures may have been influenced by her past experience. Instead of recognizing that the raised voices she hears in these meetings indicate strong feelings about the subjects under discussion, she feels that they are personally threatening. It is possible that her perception of the situation is shaped by early associations, when loud adult voices made her feel anxious and helpless. Without realizing it, Vicky is letting childhood feelings and memories influence her adult behaviour in a way that increases the pressure she feels and lowers her self-esteem. Because of this, team meetings are occasions that generate stress for her.

Exercise 26

Think about the messages you received as a child and when you were growing up. In the left-hand column below are topics about which you may have received strong suggestions, perhaps about the way to behave and what was expected of you. In the right-hand column, jot down what those ideas were. At the top of both columns is an example of the kind of message that is given to children.

Topic	*Messages*
Success	You should succeed at everything you try.

Success ....

Pleasing other people ....

Being independent ....

Arguments ....

Behaving quietly ....

Being kind ....

Danger/safety ....

Behaving noisily ....

Putting yourself first ....

Doing your best ....

Being careful ....

Having a go ....

Being helpful ....

Being a leader ....

Money ....

Getting attention ....

Getting things done quickly ....

Working long hours ....

Being obedient ....

Joking/playing around ....

Not making a fuss ....

Exercise 27

Look at the messages you have identified and think about how they affect your behaviour now. You may see their effects in things you say and do, the relationships you have, decisions you have made, what you tell your own children, perhaps, about how they should live. Try to find precise examples and list these below. These will enable you to see clearly how these messages have become underlying attitudes that inform your behaviour in different areas of your life.

Message   *How it influences me*

Exercise 28

It may be that some of the messages and behaviours you identified above are healthy and positive, but it is very likely that some of them are unhelpful and contribute to stressful experiences. Look carefully at the beliefs directly concerned with you yourself, ideas you have about the kind of person you are and the qualities you have, and list them below.

Message about myself   *Who gave it*   *How I felt*

41

Look first at the negative messages. Have you absorbed criticism and comments that then act as self-fulfilling prophecies — that is you behave in a way that reinforces those messages? Look at the people who gave the messages. Are they all people you respect and admire, whose opinion matters to you today? Are these beliefs about yourself contributing to harmful stress, keeping you tense and aroused, with low self-confidence and self-esteem?

Look now at the positive messages. If none of the ones you listed is positive, make a new list. Think about how you would feel if the positive beliefs dominated, were strong enough to drive out or keep in perspective the negative.

Exercise 29

First, on a sheet of paper, list the negative messages about yourself that you wish to change. Burn the paper.

Second, take the positive statements and write them down. Repeat them to yourself.

Self-persuasion and self-talk are ways into changing beliefs, and it is in your power to alter your beliefs and your perceptions to develop the confidence and self-acceptance that contribute to a stress-tolerant way of life.

Exercise 30

Think about the situations that cause you stress. You might like to begin with those you identified in Exercise 3 (page 2) or with any others you prefer. Try to trace a link between these and a value, attitude or belief you have always thought important. An example is given of such a link — add your own below it.

Situation	Belief
An argument with your daughter or son.	Good parents don't get angry with their children.

You have now begun to identify some unhelpful ideas that are preventing you from turning negative experiences into positive ones. At the end of this series of exercises, you will practise ways of replacing unhelpful messages from the past with positive ones that will enable you to meet the challenge of stress with vigour and optimism.

First, though, take some time to consider in more detail your present attitudes and responses. We can create stress for ourselves in ways we hardly realize; recognizing and acknowledging these is an essential first step, but often a very difficult one to take. As you saw at the beginning of this chapter, change, in itself, is stressful and sometimes we find all kinds of reasons for not changing. Sometimes we are scared of the ramifications the change will bring. Sometimes other people's ideas and expectations are challenged by our changing and they may not support it. But, understanding ourselves and how we create harmful stress for ourselves will enable us to become more aware of our own stressors and more confident about our ability to change and control our responses.

'Shoulds' and 'oughts'

Different people have different ways of coping with crises. Sometimes our reactions and our ways of responding are conditioned by ingrained ideas about how we should behave. Think about a recent situation you found stressful and, using it as a base, examine your usual way of reacting in similar circumstances.

Reaction	Yes	No
I put on a brave face.	☐	☐
I behave as if nothing has happened.	☐	☐
I look for sympathy.	☐	☐
I keep my feelings to myself.	☐	☐
I imagine how things might have turned out.	☐	☐
I try not to think about it.	☐	☐
I get angry with the people or things that caused the problem.	☐	☐
I go on as if nothing has happened.	☐	☐
I avoid being with people.	☐	☐
I wish I could change what happened.	☐	☐

If you ticked the 'No' boxes for the third and seventh reactions and 'Yes' boxes for all the others, it is possible that your behaviour is conditioned by the belief that showing your feelings or looking for sympathy and support are signs of weakness. This belief, though, prevents you from dealing effectively with pressure and crisis because people who do talk about their feelings, allow themselves to be angry and acknowledge their emotions generally cope better with them. The idea that you should put a brave face on things and that you ought not to be upset is making you less able to deal with the situation. Giving vent to your feelings with someone you trust (and who can take it!) is not only reassuring, it has been shown to protect people in crisis from experiencing the mental and physical illnesses suffered by those unable to behave in this way.

Exercise 31

You can change your beliefs about this aspect of your behaviour. You can begin by altering your way of thinking, and replacing statements about what you used to think with statements about what you can think from now on. List below the ideas you have inherited about the 'shoulds' and 'oughts' of admitting your feelings, then list beside them your new ideas (the first is an example of the kind of positive change you can make).

Past belief   *Future belief*

I shouldn't show my feelings.   I can show my feelings if I choose to.

Scenario 7

Diane was in tears when Roy arrived home. He took one look at her and said, 'You didn't get it, then?'

Diane shook her head. 'No,' she said, 'Jim's got it. I suppose I'm glad for him really — and I've got to admit he'll do the job well.' She blew her nose noisily and burst out, 'It's just so unfair! I work much harder than he does. I'm always first in the building and the last to leave, and I never miss a deadline. He's often late with things, I know, and he leaves right on the dot. I've seen him speeding off down the road when I'm still working.'

She took a shuddering breath and wailed again, 'It's just not fair!'

Diane believes that hard work should be rewarded. Many of us may have grown up believing that the way to success is to be seen working longer hours than anyone else, for example. With this goes the unconscious belief that other people should acknowledge our efforts and that we should be rewarded. These beliefs make us very vulnerable to pressure, but we can alter our perception of this issue and create a more helpful way of looking at it.

Exercise 32

Think about the beliefs you have about the 'shoulds' and 'oughts' of hard work and reward. You may be able to change some of them right away; there may be some you would just like to question. Identify your unhelpful ideas below, then begin to look at them differently.

Past belief   *Future belief*

Exercise 33

Think of all the 'shoulds', 'oughts', and 'musts' in your life. Separate them into those concerned with work and those concerned with your family or personal life.

ARE YOU STRESS-PRONE?

Home/family

Family life ought to be ....

With my kids I should ....

Other ....

....

....

Social/personal life

I should ....

Other ....

....

....

....

....

At work

Work should be ....

Other ....

....

....

....

Now go through what you have written and ask yourself if these beliefs are *always* true, if you always want to behave according to them. Remember you have a choice. With each statement, write down the opposite and indicate to yourself the fact that choice is possible. For example:

I should cook a meal every evening.	I need not cook a meal *every* evening. I can choose whether to or not.

Messages for the future

As you have seen, unhelpful mental attitudes can be altered and replaced with positive messages for the future. One way of doing this is to examine the way you 'talk' to yourself about personal stressful situations. We all experience an inner dialogue. We tell ourselves things about people and situations, and sometimes our inner dialogue is negative — anticipating failure and playing down success. We tell ourselves things like, 'It's no good, I won't be able to do it', or, 'I'm dreading the meeting/interview/party'. We can, however, make a conscious effort to talk to ourselves in a confident and positive way, one that anticipates success and relishes challenge.

Scenario 8

'Aren't you ready yet?', David called from downstairs.

'Won't be a minute', Margot replied, and continued to sit on the edge of the bed, staring at herself in the mirror. She noticed that her face was flushed and her mouth dry. No one realized how much she hated this kind of social gathering. She always felt that everyone was looking at her and finding fault with her appearance and she never knew what to say to people. Who would want to talk to her anyway, she was so dull and uninteresting. Everyone else seemed to have such interesting jobs and such full lives. No wonder she spent hours in the bathroom on these occasions.

'Actually,' she called out, 'I've got an awful migraine. It's probably better if I don't go.'

David's furious face appeared in the doorway.

Margot's inner dialogue is negative. Her thoughts all focus on ideas that reflect a sense of threat and indicate mistaken unhelpful ideas. She says to herself:

'People aren't interested in me.'
'I'm not worth knowing.'
'Everyone is criticizing me.'
'I have nothing to say.'

Margot could change the messages she gives herself. She could calm herself down by making statements that help her to interpret the situation positively and realistically. She could say to herself:

47

'Does it *matter* if some of the people there aren't interested in me? I have family and friends who are involved with me — these are only people with whom I'm socializing for the evening.'
'It isn't likely that every single one of them will look at me critically.'
'What's the worst thing that could happen at this party?'

By thinking *this* way, Margot is making her inner dialogue positive and helpful. She is talking to herself in a way that will help to calm her down and see the stressful situation in a different light. She is actually taking the threat out of the situation by changing her perception of it and reinforcing the change with statements she can hear in her head.

Exercise 34

Examine your own inner dialogue in stressful situations. Take one of the circumstances you have already identified, or a new one if you like — perhaps something you are facing at the moment. It may be a deadline to meet or an exam or an interview.

Listen to what you say to yourself about it. Identify what you say about what is happening, what it means, what will happen next . . . listen to your self-talk and self-instructions. Put into words precisely what you are fearing. Be aware of the images that cross your mind.

Repeat the exercise a few times with different situations and write them down below.

Situation   *Negative inner dialogue*

Now repeat the process, but change your *negative* self-talk to *positive*, *calming*, *realistic* statements.

Situation   *Positive inner dialogue*

Another way in which you can create positive messages for the future is by visualizing and imagining yourself coping successfully in a situation you perceive as stressful. Our mental images and fantasies are extremely powerful and exert enormous influence. In the first part of the previous exercise you may have been aware of how strong are our images of threat and hostility, but these can be replaced by equally strong images of success and effectiveness.

In the following exercise, you will see yourself reaching your goal, behaving in the way you would like to behave. You will be doing more than just *watching* yourself doing this, you will be actually *experiencing* yourself doing it, actually feeling the emotions involved.

Exercise 35

First, choose one of the situations you have already looked at in terms of unhelpful beliefs and negative inner dialogue.

Second, find somewhere to lie down and relax. (You may like to use some of the relaxation techniques described on pages 123–26.) Take five or ten minutes to become calm and free from tension.

Third, visualize the situation. You may find it helpful to write notes in reply to the following questions.

Where are you? ....

Are you sitting, standing, lying? ....

What can you feel? ....

What can you see? ....

What can you hear? ....

What can you smell? ....

Are other people present? ....

Where are they? ....

What are they doing? ....

How are they behaving towards you? ....

How do you feel? ....

What is your body doing? ....

Fourth, allow yourself to feel the anxiety you associate with the situation. What is beginning to happen to you?

Fifth, interrupt the process. Relax into the scene. Decide what you want to happen. Visualize yourself behaving as you would like to. Imagine the response of the other(s).

Sixth, stop visualizing. Relax for a minute.

How did it go? If there was anything you weren't happy with, run it through again until you perfect the style you want to use and get the results that please you. Change anything you don't like.

The whole time, be aware of how you feel. If at the end you don't feel happy and comfortable with yourself, make changes until you do.

When you are satisfied with what you've got, run the scene through four or five times.

It should take about 30 to 60 seconds to complete a scene.

If this doesn't work or if there is a situation you find particularly difficult, follow the same procedure but just visualize the scene for longer.

Allow yourself to remain in the stressful situation (the fourth step) for eight minutes, staying as calm as possible. Every 30 seconds or so, use positive inner dialogue, telling yourself not to worry. Don't move on to seeing yourself cope, just keep exposing your feelings to the perceived threat.

When you feel ready, briefly visualize the satisfactory outcome.

If you practise this technique, you should find that your perception of the situation has altered. You have replaced harmful ideas with positive ones and strengthened your ability to meet the challenge of pressure.

The previous exercises have enabled you to *think* and *feel* yourself into a new way of behaving. Another way to forge strong and helpful attitudes to replace your old ones is to *act* yourself into a new way of thinking and feeling. It is very important that new *messages* should be linked to new *behaviour* in some way. A shift in *attitude* means that you will *behave* differently in situations you find stressful.

Exercise 36

You are now going to practise behaving differently for a given period of time.

Choose a pattern of behaviour you feel contributes to stress in your life. It might be your tendency to put things off until the last minute, for example, or need to finish everything perfectly. Write it down below.

My .... contributes to stress in my life.

Now, imagine yourself behaving in an entirely opposite way in every situation where this tendency appears.

For a week, behave in the opposite way.

Play the part of someone who never puts things off or leaves things unfinished or imperfectly finished. Every day, note the changes you made below.

Day   *Different behaviour*
1

2

3

4

5

6

7

By throwing yourself into a different way of behaving, you have had a powerful experience of a potentially more rewarding approach. Action has effectively reinforced your positive thinking, talking and preparing for change.

You are now better equipped to behave differently in the specific stressful situations you encounter and to respond to them as challenges rather than threats.

3

Dealing with people

Ways of behaving

Much of the unwelcome stress in our lives comes from our dealings with other people. Life consists of a series of conflicts with others, some major, some trivial. 'Conflict' in this context does not necessarily mean fighting or hostility, but, rather, the inevitable differences of opinion we experience in our relationships with other people. These differences can range from bitter arguments on matters of principle to minor disagreements about which film to see, but all can cause us distress and discomfort.

Despite this, life without differences, without conflict, would be dull and bland. Furthermore, conflict can be healthy and stimulating. It can be constructive and developmental, enabling us to grow in knowledge of ourselves and of others. At one time it was thought that conflict was bad, something to be avoided, and people known to engage in it were seen as troublemakers. More recently, conflict has been seen as an essential element in relationships — if it is handled effectively. It can be a point of growth and development. If we recognize the real nature of the conflict we are experiencing, we can grow in understanding of ourselves and the others involved and move towards greater understanding.

Many arguments are not actually about what appear to be the issues. They are about underlying values, beliefs, ideas about the world and our roles in it. For example, an argument about being late home may not be about the number of minutes late, but about someone's unreliability or someone's feelings about being taken for granted or dissatisfaction with roles within the relationship. Identifying the core of the conflict is an important step, and a much more positive move than ignoring it or wasting energy arguing about surface matters.

Conflict can lead to change and innovation — indeed, it may be said that it actively encourages growth and change. It can bring out all our hidden resources of energy and motivation as new ideas emerge and stimulate discussion. At best, conflict can lead to open and constructive exploration of feelings and attitudes.

Often, however, conflict is unpleasant and destructive and a major source of stress in our lives. It causes us to experience hurt feelings, frustration, anger. Some of these negative feelings are caused not by the situation itself but by the way we deal with it and the way we respond to the person or people involved. However, your response to many situations

53

can be controlled and managed so that the stress of conflict can be helpful, stimulating and developmental. Although we are programmed for 'fight or flight', as mentioned earlier, these instinctive reactions can be governed. We can learn to manage our behaviour and replace unhelpful ways of responding with ways that reduce harmful pressure and enhance our dignity and self-esteem.

In any situation, there are choices open to us, but often they are choices we don't exercise. We may have fallen into certain modes of behaviour and response, not realizing that we are locking ourselves into damaging and unproductive habits, and are unaware of the idea that there are different ways of behaving and that an alternative way might be more appropriate and could help to reduce the pressure we place on ourselves.

Exercise 37

Consider what your likely response would be in the following situations and put a tick in the box by the statement that most closely matches what you would do.

1 A friend has borrowed some money from you and has not yet paid it back. Do you:

☐ a) tackle him about it in public, saying you've waited long enough

☐ b) drop hints about how hard up you are

☐ c) forget about it — it's annoying, but you'd find it embarrassing to bring it up

☐ d) in private, tell him you were pleased to lend the money and now you need it back.

2 Your child is ill and both you and your partner have work commitments. Your partner assumes you will stay at home. Do you:

☐ a) feel annoyed and taken for granted, but agree

☐ b) say, 'Why should it be me? He/she's your child too'

☐ c) explain why it is particularly difficult for you on this day and ask your partner to alter their arrangements

☐ d) say, 'OK, but it'll be your fault if I lose that order'.

3 You are in the supermarket and in a hurry. Just as it's your turn at the till, someone says, 'Do you mind if I go first — I've only got a few items?' Do you:

☐ a) say you realize they've only a few items, but you've waited a long time and are in a hurry

☐ b) feel irritated, but let the person go first

☐ c) tell them they've got a nerve trying to push in

☐ d) let them in, then tap your foot impatiently and comment on how long you've waited.

4 A friend you work with asks you if you can give them a lift home every evening from now on. You don't want to do this. Do you:

☐ a) say 'Isn't it time you passed your driving test/bought a car?'

☐ b) say you'd like to, but it would be a bit difficult because sometimes you stop off for some shopping and you don't always leave at the same time . . .

☐ c) say you appreciate the person's situation, but you don't want to be tied down to giving them a lift every day.

☐ d) leave bus and train timetables on their desk.

5 You ask a friend to the cinema, and they ask someone else along. You don't dislike this person, but you had wanted an evening for two. Do you:

☐ a) say that's fine by you, and feel resentful all evening

☐ b) tell your friend you'd appreciate it if your original plans were adhered to

☐ c) agree, but show your displeasure by freezing the third person out of the conversation

☐ d) tell your friend that you like the other person but would prefer it to be just the two of you on this occasion.

6 At work, a colleague is commended for something that was your idea. Do you:

☐ a) put the mistake right in a good-humoured way

☐ b) say, 'Actually, that was *my* idea'

☐ c) feel too embarrassed to claim the credit and wait for your colleague to speak

☐ d) say nothing, but get your own back on your colleague by subtly criticizing one of their reports.

Scoring:

1	a) W	b) X	c) Y	d) Z	4	a) W	b) Y	c) Z	d) X
2	a) Y	b) W	c) Z	d) X	5	a) Y	b) W	c) X	d) Z
3	a) Z	b) Y	c) W	d) X	6	a) Z	b) W	c) Y	d) X

Add up the number of W, X, Y and Z answers you ticked.

If your answers were mainly W, your behaviour tends towards the *aggressive*. If they were mainly X, you tend to use *manipulative* behaviour. If your answers were mainly Y, your behaviour tends to be *passive*. If you answered mainly Z, you use *assertive* behaviour in many situations.

Study sheet 7

Our behaviour can be placed in the broad categories identified above. Each style of behaviour has its advantages and disadvantages and it is helpful to differentiate between the styles to enable you to choose which is the most appropriate in a particular situation.

Aggressive behaviour sends out the message that your rights are more important than other people's. It is an attacking mode of behaviour that is directed towards putting other people down by being threatening, domineering, hostile, attacking. The goal of such behaviour is to win and to dominate and it implies that you are in some way superior to the other person.

Manipulative behaviour is a form of aggression. It is behaviour that *appears* to respect others but in fact puts them down. The goal of manipulative behaviour is to win by using such strategies as flattery, veiled hints, saying one thing and meaning another. It is based on dishonesty and its implication is that you are superior to the other person, although you disguise this.

Passive behaviour sends out the message that you have no rights and your feelings and needs are less important than other people's. It is behaviour that is compliant and submissive and its goal is to please others and avoid unpleasantness at all costs. It implies that you are in some way inferior to the other person and so your needs are not as valid.

Assertive behaviour is based on respect for yourself and your rights and for other people and their rights. It implies that you and the other person are equal as people and that you can state clearly your needs and beliefs without diminishing yourself or anyone else. Its message is one of openness. The goal of assertive behaviour is not to win, but to find solutions that encompass the needs of both parties and do not compromise anyone's self-respect.

We probably all display different degrees of aggressive, manipulative, passive and assertive behaviour at different times. These terms are not used to describe our characters or our personalities, but are ways of describing styles of interpersonal communication. They describe not what we *are* but what we *do*. Although we all use these different behaviours at different points, many of us do not differentiate between the different styles or recognize which one we are using at a particular time and it is possible that, without realizing it, we become stuck in a certain type of behaviour, or combination of behaviours, that is unhelpful and contributes towards harmful stress in our lives. We may find it hard to respond in another way, particularly when under pressure, and we may be building up tension instead of reducing it.

An ability to use different styles of behaviour according to circumstances is a valuable asset that enables us to meet a variety of stressful situations with confidence. In the majority of situations, in the long run, assertive behaviour is the most positive option and the one most likely to empower you to deal with stress and pressure confidently. A low level of assertiveness is one of the characteristics most likely to predispose a person to experiencing increased levels of stress. People who have difficulty expressing their wishes and beliefs and who have not found a way of limiting others' demands on them are more likely to experience a harmful degree of pressure than those who can assert their thoughts and feelings. The way we communicate with others and the quality of the relationships we experience can be important factors in the development of stress. The skill of assertiveness is at the heart of healthy interpersonal communication.

Being aggressive

Scenario 9

'Was it you in the stockroom yesterday?' Marion Palmer said as she strode into the office and marched over to Grant Robertson's desk. She towered over him, hands on hips. Heads were turned as Grant answered defensively, 'Yes, why?'

Marion's voice rose an octave or two. 'I'll tell you why. I've never seen the place in such a mess! It looked as if a battle had gone on in there. You may have trouble following simple systems, but you could at least clear up after you. It took me 20 minutes to find what I wanted and, unlike *some* people, I've got more than enough to do.' She turned on her heel and left Grant looking sheepish and embarrassed, oblivious of the sympathetic glances thrown in his direction. He wasn't the only one to have been at the receiving end of Marion's outbursts.

Her raised voice was heard again later in the day. 'It's a ridiculous idea!' she exclaimed in reply to Don Blackett's proposal for a new system for dealing with customer complaints. Her fingers tapped on the table to emphasize her point. 'There's absolutely nothing wrong with the way we're doing it at the moment and there are quite enough changes to contend with as it is. I want to get on with something much more urgent — the arrangements for Brian's leaving do. I don't want another fiasco like the Christmas outing.' A frown creased her forehead. 'So, I've decided that. . . .' Everyone sat in uncomfortable silence as Marion outlined the arrangements she had drawn up without reference to them.

It was a great pity, Grant thought, that Marion antagonized them so much that they ignored any truth in what she said. She was right about not making any more changes; the new manager would be quite enough to cope with, and it was true that a lot had gone wrong with the Christmas outing. But Grant, for one, felt only resentment as Marion catalogued the mishaps, insisting that none was her fault. 'It's too bad,' she was saying, 'when you've spent the hours I had planning everything meticulously, only to be let down by the coach company's total inefficiency. I told them, believe me. . . .'

Everyone sitting round the table had no difficulty believing that she had told them and none felt a flicker of sympathy.

Marion's behaviour is aggressive. She is full of anger and attack, creating conflict in most situations.

She makes decisions for other people without considering their needs or priorities. Her approach is pushy and threatening. She is critical of other people, dismissing and ridiculing those who hold different opinions, but she does not admit to her own mistakes or faults. She often interrupts people or doesn't give them time to reply.

Marion's non-verbal behaviour also speaks of aggression. Her posture is strained and tense. She tends to clench her fists, point her finger and stand with arms crossed or hands on her hips. Her facial expression is usually frowning or angry and she stares other people down. Her voice is strident and inappropriately loud and often sounds cold or sarcastic.

Why does Marion behave in this way?

Sometimes aggression hides a lack of confidence. When you feel under stress or threatened, it is easy to lose confidence in yourself and you may try to hide this by being aggressive. Some aggressive people have a low opinion of themselves. Sometimes aggression springs from anxiety. Newly promoted people, for example, can be aggressive at first in their dealings with others.

Perhaps aggressive role models have provided an example. Aggression may be seen as part of being successful. Also, if you have been at the receiving end of aggression from authority figures, such as parents or bosses, you may behave aggressively towards people junior to you.

Exercise 38

Examine the following statements and, on a scale of one to ten (ten being the highest) tick the number that corresponds to how strongly you hold the belief.

	1	2	3	4	5	6	7	8	9	10
I believe you shouldn't let people push you around.	☐	☐	☐	☐	☐	☐	☐	☐	☐	☐
Getting my own way is important to me.	☐	☐	☐	☐	☐	☐	☐	☐	☐	☐
You can't be successful *and* nice.	☐	☐	☐	☐	☐	☐	☐	☐	☐	☐
You have to show people who's boss.	☐	☐	☐	☐	☐	☐	☐	☐	☐	☐
It's best to get in first before you're criticized.	☐	☐	☐	☐	☐	☐	☐	☐	☐	☐
When you know you're right, there's nothing wrong with forcing others to agree with you.	☐	☐	☐	☐	☐	☐	☐	☐	☐	☐
There are only winners and losers and I'm not going to be a loser.	☐	☐	☐	☐	☐	☐	☐	☐	☐	☐

Add up the numbers you have ticked.

If you score between 58 and 70, your beliefs and attitudes are probably causing you to behave very aggressively, and it is very likely that this behaviour pattern is causing you to experience harmful stress.

Exercise 39

Think about a situation in which you displayed aggressive behaviour, then describe it using the following headings.

Situation: ....

....

What I said: ....

....

....

How I said it: ....

....

....

What I did (gestures, etc.): ....

....

....

What my body felt like: ....

....

....

What emotions I felt: ....

....

....

What reaction I got from other people: ....

....

....

What the outcome was: ....

....

Now re-run the situation and make some changes. Alter the words you used, changing any demanding or attacking phrases. Change your aggressive body language, and note the difference in the way your body feels when you relax your jaws and shoulders, for example. Imagine the different emotions you might feel as a result, and the different reactions and outcome.

Exercise 40

Now think of a situation you will be experiencing in the near future in which you know you are likely to respond aggressively. Building on the previous exercise, imagine yourself behaving differently from usual.

Situation: ....

....

What I will say: ....

....

....

How I will say it: ....

....

....

What I will do: ....

....

....

What my body will feel like: ....

....

....

What emotions I will feel: ....

....

....

How other people may react: ....

....

....

What the outcome may be: ....

....

....

You may find that the outcome is not one you want. Faced with a less aggressive approach, people may not give in to you so readily. However, you are exchanging the short-term gains of getting your own way and feeling you are winning for the long-term advantages of experiencing more mutual respect in relationships. You are moving towards seeing problems with situations and people as *problems*, not *threats*, and are beginning to practise behaviour that enables you to deal with conflict in a positive, stress-free way.

Being manipulative

Scenario 10

Geoff Bradley reviewed his first term as principal with satisfaction. He'd had some tricky members of staff to deal with, but he'd brought them round to his way of thinking. He thought he'd managed to do it without, dare he say, sacrificing too much popularity. Of course, you can't expect to be *popular* when you're the boss, but it's still good to feel that you're *liked*.

He was pleased with the way he'd put through some major changes without alienating the staff involved. He had found that the trick was to ask for their opinions, listen to them very intently (that management course on body language was invaluable), then subtly bring them round to his own way of thinking, so that the final decision seemed to be theirs. It always seemed to work.

It always helped to praise people, too — a bit of ego-boosting never hurt. Even something vague like, 'You're doing a splendid job in the department' would do and would soften the forthcoming blow. Never easy, moving people in directions they're unwilling to take. Still, let's face it, when you know what you're going to do anyway it doesn't really matter what you say to keep people happy.

Now and again, he had felt a little uneasy about the way he'd handled something. The same approach didn't work for everyone. He'd been a bit twinkly and flirtatious with the new Business Studies woman and it seemed to thaw her initial reserve, but it had been entirely different when he'd told Jo Cousins that she was going to have to teach Information Technology next year. He'd walked her to the door and put his hand on her shoulder in what he thought was a friendly manner and made some joky remark about swapping a cooker for a computer. She had looked at him very coldly and later he'd thought he heard her mutter to a colleague something about a patronizing so-and-so, but perhaps he'd misheard.

Well, never mind, he'd got his own way easily on most matters. He stretched himself out in a relaxed posture as a knock came at the door.

'Come in, Bill', he said fulsomely.

Geoff's behaviour is manipulative. He *appears* to treat people with respect and to take their opinions into account, but in reality he is riding roughshod over them and making sure that things happen the way he *wants* them to. He can be two-faced, praising insincerely to get what he wants. His manner is often flirtatious or patronizing. Sometimes, he puts people down in the guise of joking, flippant remarks. Geoff's body language conveys his manipulative approach. His posture is deliberately relaxed and he uses touching or patting to convey friendliness. In the same way, his tone of voice is exaggeratedly amiable. Some in-built aggression may be detected in a hint of sarcasm or his too-strong handshake or slap on the back.

Why does Geoff behave like this?

Manipulative behaviour can stem from lack of confidence, which causes him to boost his self-esteem by controlling other people more subtly than by aggressive means. The need to be in control and the desire to be liked are underlying factors of this type of behaviour.

People who use manipulative means to get their way may be basing their behaviour on role models they have observed or who have influenced them in the past. They may be copying the kinds of tactics that others have employed towards them.

Exercise 41

Examine the following statements and, on a scale of one to ten (ten being the highest) tick the number that corresponds with how strongly you hold this belief.

1 2 3 4 5 6 7 8 9 10

It is good to flatter people, even if what you praise them for doesn't really apply to them.

People who are seen as charming or flirtatious are liked and get on with others.

A good way of getting out of things you don't want to do is to 'forget' to do them or to make excuses for not doing them.

It is important to let other people *think* you agree with them/ approve of them even if you don't.

People won't like you unless you agree with them.

Paying lip-service to other people's views saves unpleasantness.

Making people feel guilty is an effective way of getting them to do what you want.

Add up all the numbers you have ticked. If you scored between 58 and 70, your attitudes and beliefs are probably causing you to behave manipulatively. While you may feel that this mode of behaviour is effective and harmless, it eventually destroys trust and increases tension as you become locked into playing games with other people.

Exercise 42

Think of a situation when you displayed manipulative behaviour, then describe it using the following headings.

Situation: ....

....

....

What I said: ....

....

....

How I said it: ....

....

....

What I did (gestures, etc.): ....

....

....

What my body felt like: ....

....

....

What emotions I felt: ....

....

....

What reactions I got from other people: ....

....

....

What the outcome was: ....

....

Now re-run the situation and make some changes. Look at the words and phrases you used and replace them with more open expressions. Think how you could change your body language. Position yourself differently, alter the gestures you used.

Exercise 43

Now think of a situation you will experience in the near future in which you know you are likely to behave manipulatively. Building on the previous exercise, imagine yourself behaving differently and write down the changes you would make below.

Situation: ....

....

What I will say: ....

....

....

How I will say it: ....

....

....

What I will do (gestures, etc.): ....

....

....

What my body will feel like: ....

....

....

What emotions I will feel: ....

....

....

How other people may react: ....

....

....

What the outcome might be: ....

....

You may find that the outcome is not what you want. Other people may be more open with you as a result of your more honest behaviour and it may be difficult to adjust to this at first. However, you are moving towards building more self-respect and more mutual respect in your dealings with other people and, in the long term, you will reduce the pressure and stress that accompany manipulative game-playing.

Being passive

Scenario 11

Jane Godfrey stood miserably on the railway station, a bag weighed down with shopping clutched between her ankles. It was already six o'clock and there was not a sign of the train.

If only she hadn't let Clive use the car that morning. Well, she hadn't really 'let' him, he had just said, 'It's OK if I take the car today, isn't it? Pete can't give me the usual lift', and was outside the door as she was saying, 'Well, I suppose so, but the train journey is awfully incon-venient, especially as I've got to get the stuff for tonight . . .'.

Her voice had died away, just as it had done earlier when Sue had said, 'You won't mind working an extra hour, will you, to get this finished? You can take the time next week.' Jane had started to say, 'Well, actually, I'm afraid . . .', but Sue had gone. 'Honestly!' she complained to Tasheen over their mid-morning coffee, 'Sue's always pulling that kind of trick — well, she is on me, anyway. And I bet you she'll forget about my having the extra time next week.'

'Why don't you remind her?', said Tasheen. He was finding Jane very irritating and hard to work with these days. She never seemed to say what she wanted — just relied on people to guess — then crept round with a defeated expression on her face. 'Oh, I won't bother,' said Jane heroically, 'you know Sue, she can be a bit funny. No, I don't mind, really — anything for a quiet life.'

'She's just got herself to blame,' thought Tasheen, 'she brings out the bully in people like Sue.'

At last, the train pulled into the station. Jane clambered on and thought, 'The one good thing that's happened today — a free window seat in a non-smoking compartment'. She settled herself and her shopping comfortably.

As the train pulled out, the young lad opposite her lit up a cigarette and exhaled a long plume of smoke. Jane sighed to herself and spent the journey with her face averted and held her breath.

Jane's behaviour is passive or submissive. She doesn't stand up for her rights as a person but, rather, allows herself to be trampled upon. She doesn't state clearly what she wants and she puts her own needs last. Confrontation or argument disturbs and distresses her, so she backs away from it.

Jane doesn't express anger or strong feelings and she lets herself be forced into situations. She often says 'Yes' when she means to say 'No'.

Her non-verbal behaviour reinforces this message of submissiveness. Her posture is often slumped and she stays at a low level, sitting when the other person is standing. She fidgets a lot — touching her face constantly or fiddling with a bit of her hair. She finds it hard to look directly at people. Her facial expression is either fed-up and defeated or she has a nervous, eager-to-please smile.

Jane's voice is quiet and hesitant, as if she is apologizing for speaking at all.

Why does Jane behave like this?

Sometimes passive behaviour stems from lack of confidence and lack of self-respect. When you feel under stress or threatened, your instinctive response is to take flight rather than fight. It is possible that Jane has been influenced by submissive role models who gave her the message that other people should always be put before oneself and that to ask for anything for oneself is pushy and unacceptable behaviour.

Exercise 44

Examine the following statements and, on a scale of one to ten (ten being the highest), tick the number that corresponds to how strongly you hold this belief.

1 2 3 4 5 6 7 8 9 10

It is selfish to ask for what you want.

Other people's needs should always come first.

I need to feel liked by others.

Rows and unpleasantness should be avoided.

It is wrong to make a fuss about your own feelings.

It is often better to agree to or put up with things just to keep the peace.

Anger should be kept to oneself.

Add up the numbers you have ticked. If you scored between 58 and 70, your beliefs and attitudes are probably causing you to behave very passively or submissively and it is very likely that this pattern of behaviour is causing you to experience harmful stress.

Exercise 45

Think about a situation when you displayed passive behaviour and describe it using the following headings.

Situation: ....

....

What I said: ....

....

....

How I said it: ....

....

....

....

What I did (gestures, etc.): ....

....

....

What my body felt like: ....

....

....

What emotions I felt: ....

....

....

What reactions I got from other people: ....

....

....

What the outcome was: ....

....

Now re-run the situation and make some changes. Look at the words and phrases you used and replace them with less apologetic expressions. Make your gestures and your posture more definite and positive. Notice the increased confidence that comes simply from adopting an upright posture and a firmer tone of voice.

Exercise 46

Think of a situation you will be experiencing in the near future in which you are likely to behave passively. Building on the previous exercise, imagine yourself behaving differently and write the changes you would make below.

DEALING WITH PEOPLE

Situation: ....

....

What I will say: ....

....

....

How I will say it: ....

....

....

What I will do (gestures, etc.): ....

....

....

What my body will feel like: ....

....

....

What emotions I will feel: ....

....

....

How other people may react: ....

....

....

What the outcome may be: ....

....

It is possible that the result will be different from the one you want. Passive behaviour can protect you from blame. It can lead to your being generally seen as a good sort, reliable and unselfish. However, by examining your behaviour and its underlying attitudes and beginning to make some changes, you are moving towards a more positive style of behaviour. Exchanging the short-term pay-off of avoiding conflict and being regarded as nice for the long-term benefits of more confident and open behaviour will enable you to deal with stress and pressure much more effectively.

Being assertive

Scenario 12

Helen arrived home, tired after the long meeting with Trevor, but pleased with its outcome and looking forward to telling Gareth about it over a nice supper and a bottle of wine. The kids were going out —Emma to babysit for a neighbour and Mark to his Venture Scouts group.

Emma met her at the door with a 'Bye, Mum, see you later'.

Through the open kitchen door, Helen could see dirty dishes and cooking utensils piled high. 'Wait a minute,' she said, 'what about this lot?'

Emma sighed impatiently, 'There isn't time to clear up — sorry. I've got to be there at seven.'

'Where's Mark?'

Emma shrugged, 'Upstairs getting ready. Look Mum, I'm really late now . . . .'

'You can wait for a minute or two.'

Helen was angry and fed up. The last thing she felt like facing was a messy kitchen and this kind of thing had happened all too often recently.

Mark's face appeared over the banister. 'What's up?' he said.

Helen took a deep breath. 'I want to speak to you both for a minute.'

Emma and Mark exchanged grimaces and waited to hear what Helen had to say.

'You two know you are expected to clear up after yourselves and to help with the chores.' She kept her voice calm and looked at them steadily. 'I'm feeling fed up and angry that I've come home tonight to this mess. I would like one of you to clear it up now and for the two of you to make a rota for sharing the chores from now on.'

When the children started complaining and squabbling about which one of them was the most late, Helen repeated firmly, 'I would like one of you to clear up the mess now', and went to have a shower.

Not only was the kitchen clean and tidy when she came down, but she was pleased that she had handled the situation without blowing her top at the children or grumbling and clearing it up herself.

'Well, how did the meeting go?' asked Gareth as he poured the wine.

'It was OK,' said Helen, 'I was nervous about telling Trevor I wanted a pay rise because of all the extra work since the office expansion, but I'm really glad now I made the appointment to go and talk about it. There would have been no point just complaining endlessly to the others or dropping hints.'

'Did he agree?' asked Gareth, 'Did you get what you asked for?'

'No,' said Helen, 'not exactly. After we'd discussed it, he said he could offer a bit less than I'd asked for, but it would be reviewed again in six months if the workload hadn't decreased. That's fine. Another good thing — I think he respected me for being straight with him about what I wanted and why. We may even get on better in the future!'

'I'll drink to that', said Gareth, and they raised their glasses in a toast.

Helen's behaviour throughout is assertive. She can identify and express her thoughts, feelings and wishes clearly and directly without threatening people, putting them down or playing games with them. This type of behaviour is most effective in dealing with people and situations that cause stress and pressure.

Study sheet 8

Assertiveness involves dealing with others directly, openly and honestly. It is not about being bossy or aggressive or getting your own way. It is not about exercising power or manipulating people.

It is a style of behaviour and an attitude to other people that stems from your own self-esteem and a belief in everyone's fundamental rights as human beings. It is about respecting your own rights and those of other people. These attitudes are expressed through clear and confident communication.

Assertive people can express their thoughts, feelings and wishes directly. They can evaluate a situation and decide how to act without being influenced by anxiety or guilt. They take responsibility for their decisions and choices.

In order to communicate what we feel about a situation and what we want to happen, we have to be clear about what we feel and know what outcome we want. This involves developing self-knowledge and a sound awareness of our feelings and attitudes. It also involves consideration for others. Assertive behaviour is based on respect for others, on listening to and acknowledging their needs and wishes. Your assertive behaviour will encourage similar behaviour in others.

Assertiveness isn't about winning all the time. It is more about negotiating life without anxiety or aggression. It is a style of response that will enable you to cope effectively with pressure and to develop a personal strength to build healthy relationships.

Exercise 47

Look back at the verbal and non-verbal language you used in your examples of your own aggressive, manipulative and passive behaviour.

Look at the changes you made. These changes should be leading you towards a more assertive style of behaviour.

Check them against the following list.

Assertive behaviour

Words/phrases
- I like . . .
- I want . . .
- I feel . . .
- Can we discuss this?

- I won't . . .
- I don't . . .
- What do you think?
- What do you feel about this?

Not
- I should . . .
- I ought . . .
- You should . . .
- You ought . . .

Body language/gestures
- Relaxed, steady posture.
- Direct eye contact.
- Open, relaxed gestures.

- Open, pleasant expression.
- Same level as other person.
- Acceptable distance from other person.

Voice
- Relaxed tone of voice.
- Medium volume.

- Low-pitched.
- Even and firm.

Exercise 48

A vital part of assertive behaviour is the underlying acceptance that you have rights and that your rights are equal to everyone else's. Some rights are listed below. Change any that do not reflect your own values and add as many to the list as you wish.

- I have the right to ask for what I want.
- I have the right to express my feelings.
- I have the right to say 'No'.

- I have the right to make mistakes.
- I have the right to change my mind.
- I have the right to ....

....

Remember, having rights does not mean you have to exercise them all the time or even in the same way. You do have the right and the ability to choose and you may choose to behave differently in different situations. A conflict with a shop assistant about faulty goods or with a customer about who is next in the queue is very different from being in disagreement with your partner about an issue arising regarding how to bring up your children, for example. But, in any situation, being confident of the rights you have identified and being practised in the skills necessary to assert them will enable you to deal with situations openly and appropriately without resorting to aggression, manipulation or passiveness.

Exercise 49

Think about the people with whom you deal in your everyday life. Some you will find more difficult than others; it may be that there are some people with whom you always feel pressurized or under stress. You may find it easy to ask a stranger to put out his cigarette because you find the smoke unpleasant, but would find it very difficult to ask someone senior to you at work to do so, for example.

First, identify the people with whom you find it difficult to assert yourself. Tick the appropriate column below.

Person	Very difficult	Quite difficult	Not difficult
Mother	☐	☐	☐
Father	☐	☐	☐
Partner/spouse	☐	☐	☐
Daughter/son	☐	☐	☐
Sister	☐	☐	☐
Brother	☐	☐	☐
Friends of same sex	☐	☐	☐
Friends of different sex	☐	☐	☐
Colleagues of equal status	☐	☐	☐

Subordinate colleagues	☐	☐	☐
Senior colleagues	☐	☐	☐
Doctors/consultants	☐	☐	☐
Waiters	☐	☐	☐
Hairdressers	☐	☐	☐
Shop assistants/managers	☐	☐	☐
Builders/repair workers, etc.	☐	☐	☐
Strangers	☐	☐	☐
Other	☐	☐	☐

With all these people, you will find it easier to assert yourself if you follow this three-step pattern:

- recognize what the problem is
- recognize how you feel
- recognize what you want to happen.

Exercise 50

You have bought a new sports bag and, after you have used it a few times, the strap breaks — just as you are on your way to a squash match. You feel annoyed and frustrated and this affects your game. You are irritated with yourself for having bought this particular brand and taking it back to the shop is particularly inconvenient this week. When you *do* get to the shop, you have to wait a long time for someone to attend to you.

Step 1
- *Identify the problem* What is the precise problem you want addressed?
- *Identify how you feel* Which of the many feelings involved in this incident are the ones you will express here?
- *Identify what you want to happen* Do you want your money back, a credit note or a replacement bag?

Step 2
Now, think about how you will communicate the above. Check the previous exercises to help you formulate a complaint that is neither aggressive nor passive. Think about appropriate posture and body language. Write down what you will do.

What I will say: ....

....

....

How I will say it: ....

....

....

You might say something like, 'I bought this bag two weeks ago and the strap has broken. I would like my money back today, please.'

Having found your formula, stick to it — even if the other person presents you with arguments. Acknowledge what they say — for example, 'Yes, I understand you haven't had any other complaints' — then go back to your request, 'but I would like my money back, please.'

Exercise 51

Choose a person you rated as 'quite difficult' in Exercise 49 and imagine a situation typical of ones you experience with this person or focus on a situation you will be experiencing. Write below what you will say to the person about how you feel and what you want and how you will say it.

Situation: ....

....

What I will say: ....

....

....

How I will say it: ....

....

....

....

What I will do (gestures, etc.): ....

....

....

What my body will feel like: ....

....

....

What emotions I will feel: ....

....

....

How the other person may react: ....

....

....

What the outcome might be: ....

....

Rehearse the whole encounter. See yourself behaving assertively. Practise aloud the tone of voice you will use, the gestures and posture you will adopt. If you feel your confidence wavering, read and re-read your list of rights (you could even learn them by heart).

Remember, you are not out to win. You are behaving in a way that will protect you from unacceptable pressure and enable you to deal effectively with stress-inducing situations.

Repeat this exercise as often as you wish. Move on to the difficult people when you feel ready, approaching each in exactly the same way.

When you have experienced the actual situation you have worked on, or one like it, jot some notes below about the encounter. These will help you to focus on what went well and what didn't and point up ways in which you can build on and learn from the experience.

Situation: ....

....

How I behaved: ....

....

....

How the other person behaved: ....

....

....

Thoughts/feelings about the incident: ....

....

....

What I learned: ....

....

....

If you behave assertively when you are under pressure:

- you will feel far better at the end of the encounter
- you are likely to have better relationships with the people involved
- you are more likely to achieve your goal or reach an acceptable compromise
- you will find that the next difficult encounter causes less pressure.

Assertive behaviour helps us, among other things, to:

- say 'No' to requests
- face constructive criticism
- face unfair criticism and put-downs
- give criticism
- deal with anger and aggression.

These topics are each covered in the following sections.

'I just can't say "No"!'

Scenario 13

'I'm glad I've bumped into you,' said Chris to Malcolm outside the supermarket on Saturday morning, 'they've roped me into helping with the hospital benefit disco next week. Will you give me a hand?'

'Well . . .', said Malcolm, 'I'm not sure . . . I'll have to see what we're doing. What night is it?'

'It's Friday,' said Chris, 'and I know you're free because I've just seen Barbara going into the hairdressers, and I checked with her! That'll be great! I'll see you up there at about seven, then.'

'Fine', said Malcolm feebly, and cursed himself all the way to the car park. He hated discos, he found them noisy and tedious and the lights hurt his eyes. The music was always rotten as well. All he wanted to do on a Friday evening after a week's work was put his feet up in front of the television. Perhaps he could make up an excuse, ring Chris during the week and say he had a stomach upset. Maybe the car could develop a last-minute fault. That would let Chris down, though, which wouldn't really be fair. He was a good bloke, did a lot for local charities. Not that Malcolm didn't want to do his bit — it was just this particular bit! He loaded the shopping into the car and drove home feeling grumpy and put-upon.

'What on earth's wrong?', asked Barbara. He told her.

'Why didn't you just say "no"?', she asked.

Malcolm looked at her. 'I just couldn't,' he said, 'Chris would think that was really off.'

'No he wouldn't,' said Barbara, 'You're only saying you don't want to help at the disco, you're not rejecting him personally!'

Malcolm thought about that for a few minutes. 'I suppose so,' he said, 'I just didn't have an excuse ready.'

'You don't need an excuse,' said Barbara, 'You can just say you don't want to do it. It's not impossible to say it nicely, you know!'

'I suppose so,' he said again, 'I just find it very hard to do. You're right, though. Tell you what, I'll do it this time, as a kind of lesson to myself, but next time I'm asked to do something I don't want to do, I'll definitely say "no".'

'Good!', said Barbara, 'how about mowing the lawn now, before it rains?'

'No,' said Malcolm, 'I don't want to do it now.'

She threw a cushion at him!

80

Malcolm doesn't say 'No' to the request to help at the disco because he feels that, as an involved member of the community, he *ought* to help. He feels guilty when he sees how much Chris does and feels it would be selfish to refuse. He likes Chris and feels that he will somehow lose standing in Chris's eyes if he doesn't agree to the request.

'No' is a very small word, but it causes many of us a lot of difficulty. We put pressure on ourselves by agreeing to things we'd rather not agree to just because we find it hard to refuse. Check your own feelings and beliefs about this issue.

Exercise 52

Read the following statements and put a tick in the column that most accurately reflects how they apply to you.

	Always	Very often	Some-times	Never
I feel guilty when I say 'No'.	☐	☐	☐	☐
I am scared to say 'No'.	☐	☐	☐	☐
If I refuse someone's request they won't like me.	☐	☐	☐	☐
If I refuse someone's request they will think less of me.	☐	☐	☐	☐
It hurts people if you say 'No'.	☐	☐	☐	☐
I hate myself for being weak when I can't say 'No'.	☐	☐	☐	☐
I end up resenting people who put me in this position.	☐	☐	☐	☐
It's difficult to know what I want or don't want.	☐	☐	☐	☐
I don't spend enough time on what I want to do.	☐	☐	☐	☐
I feel like a victim or martyr.	☐	☐	☐	☐

If you answered 'always' or 'very often' to several statements, you could be damaging your emotional health, wasting precious time and making yourself vulnerable to stress and tension.

Our inability to say 'No' is linked to several stress-connected factors. One result of agreeing to every request and suggestion is that we take on too much, agree to too many claims on our time and resources. We end up doing things that aren't important to us, leaving little time for our own interests and priorities, which *are* important to us. This could be connected with our self-image, with the idea that somehow our own needs must come after other people's. It may be that we feel we have no right to say 'No', that others are inherently superior or in a position of authority and their wishes should come first.

It is possible, however, to re-think some of your attitudes and practise refusing requests in an assertive way, which enables you to feel in control and confident because you have neither diminished yourself or the other person. As you have already discovered, beliefs and attitudes are learned and so can be unlearned and changed to provide a more positive basis for future behaviour.

Exercise 53

Re-read the list of rights and the ones you wrote down in Exercise 48 (see page 74) and decide which of them is particularly appropriate here (such as, I have the right to say 'No', I have the right to set my own priorities. Write it down here.

....

Then, take one of the statements from the previous exercise to which you answered 'always' or 'very often'. Write down another statement that challenges or contradicts or questions it (for example, there is no need to resent people who put me in this position — I put myself in this position and I can choose not to put myself in this position).

....

....

....

....

Now join the two statements. Write down the right you wish to assert, followed by a positive reinterpretation of the attitude or belief you are changing.

Repeat this exercise as often as you find helpful.

Exercise 54

We all find it easier to refuse requests from some people than from others. You may find that you have particular difficulty in saying 'No' to your boss or anyone you perceive as senior to you, but have no difficulty with equals or contemporaries. You may find it easy to say 'No' at work, but find it hard to refuse friends. It is useful to identify these differences as they will relate to areas of your life in which you may experience an unacceptable level of pressure. This exercise can help you resolve this.

In descending order of difficulty, write down the names of people to whom you find it hard to say 'No'. You could use your answers to Exercise 49 (see page 75) as the basis for this list.

Below, write down the kinds of requests you find it hard to refuse. It may be to do with your home life or your social life or your work life, your life in your community or whatever. Put them in descending order of difficulty and list as many as you find helpful.

Now, put your two lists together in as many ways as you wish. Start with the most difficult and work down (such as, I find it hard to say 'No' when my neighbour Irene asks me to babysit, I find it hard to say 'No' when my friend June asks me to help at the jumble sale, then I find it hard to say 'No' when Dennis presses another drink on me). Write them down below.

Study sheet 9

Saying 'No' assertively gets easier with practice. Consider the following guidelines:

- listen to your gut reaction — this is usually a good guide as to whether or not you really want to say 'Yes' or 'No'
- keep the reply short — don't give long, rambling excuses or justifications
- avoid the phrase 'I can't — it sounds as though you're making excuses — rather show your responsibility for your decision with a phrase like 'I won't' or 'I'm not prepared to'
- give a reason if you think it is appropriate, but don't repeat or justify it
- acknowledge the other person — show you understand what has been said and the other's feelings and position because this will make it clear you are not refusing because you haven't understood the request or because you have no regard for the person making it
- remember, you are refusing a request, not rejecting an individual
- apologize for your refusal if it's appropriate to do so, but don't overdo it
- suggest an alternative
- if you're not sure which answer to give, ask for time to decide, then say how much time you will need and how you will communicate your decision (say, I'll call you back in five minutes or I'll answer in writing by Thursday)

● don't feel guilty — you are the best judge of what you want/don't want to do.

Exercise 55

Take one of your easier examples from the previous exercise. Decide on the form of words you will use to refuse the request. Write them down here.

....

....

....

....

Decide how you will strengthen your assertive words with your body language and tone of voice. Write your description down here.

....

....

....

....

Practise saying the words out loud in the way you have described above.

Imagine what the response might be. Practise your own response to this.

Run through the scene several times until you feel familiar and comfortable with what you are saying.

Now, choose a hard example and go through the same process.

Of course, there will be times when you *want* to say 'No' but *can't*. This is part of life. But, you can learn to say 'No' in situations where it *is* possible to do so and limit the occasions you say 'Yes' to when you don't want to to the really important ones — probably those to do with duty and family. By exercising your right to say 'No' in an assertive and confident way, you are responding with honesty and integrity to demands others make of you and building up your personal resources for meeting challenge positively.

'I hate criticism!'

'You're always late!' 'Why are you so untidy?' 'The trouble with you is . . .'

No one *likes* being criticized in this way, whether the criticism is justified or not. Adverse comments about our behaviour or character often leave us feeling angry, defensive or humiliated, to such an extent that we are unwilling and unable to accept any part of the criticism, even any that is justified.

A good way of coping with criticism is to be prepared for it. You will be aware, from working through this guide, that knowledge of your own behaviour and responses provides a firm basis for understanding and managing your behaviour in stressful situations.

Being aware of your strengths and your weaknesses makes it easier for you to accept and cope with criticism from others, and to give criticism, when necessary, fairly and positively.

Exercise 56

Often we are far more aware of what we perceive to be our weaknesses rather than our strengths. Concentrate now on your strengths.

Write down as many points under the heading below as you like, including strengths you see in yourself and things others have said about you.

Good things about me

Exercise 57

Think about times when you felt good about yourself. Look at the situations and what caused the positive feelings. They may have been caused by something you achieved, or enjoyed or the feedback given to you by other people. Write down as many of them as you like.

Occasion: ....

What caused the feeling: ....

....

Look carefully at any patterns that emerge. The source of your positive feelings about yourself are the ones to cultivate and develop. The people and activities that enhance your self-esteem are your allies in your fight against unhelpful stress.

Exercise 58

In the first column below, list what you see as negative things about yourself — these might be to do with your physical appearance, your behaviour with your family or at work, habits you have.

In the second column, find something positive about each failing.

In the third column, put an A beside a quality you are prepared to accept and live with, and a C beside one you would like to change. One entry has been made to give you an example.

Negative	*Positive*	*Accept/change*
I'm lazy	I'm relaxed	C

Exercise 59

Which of the qualities you listed above are you most sensitive about? There may be one or two areas where you find criticism particularly hard to take. Rank them below, putting the ones you are most sensitive about first, and so on.

Think about an occasion when you were criticized for one of these characteristics. Try to remember what was said and how you responded, then write these points down below.

Situation: ....

....

What the other person said: ....

....

What I said: ....

....

....

What I felt: ....

....

....

It is possible that you reacted to the criticism in one of three ways:

- aggressively, because we often retaliate when we feel we're being attacked, saying things like, 'What about you, anyway?' or 'You're a fine one to talk' — counter-attack is sometimes an instinctive form of defence
- passively — to stay out of trouble and keep on the right side of the other person, you accepted what was said and vowed to keep a low profile in future
- were upset by it — sometimes we take criticism to heart, whether it is a justified complaint or not, and this is particularly the case with people whose confidence level is low as this makes us too ready to accept and absorb criticism even if we know it isn't right.

Study sheet 10

Accepting criticism in an assertive way, and so reducing its ability to create unacceptable stress, is a skill that can be learned. Read the following guidelines regarding how to behave when faced with criticism.

1 Pause. Don't react immediately. Check your body's physical response and take a deep breath to help you remain calm. Relax your shoulders and unclench your hands.
2 Listen carefully to what is said. Clarify with the speaker to check that you have understood; for example, 'You think I'm not doing my fair share of the housework'.
3 Don't respond immediately. Think if there is any truth in the criticism. Is it justified or partly justified?
4 If the criticism is true, acknowledge it without blustering or excusing yourself. Say something like, 'Yes, it's true that I haven't been doing my share recently.' If you only partly agree, make clear how far you accept the criticism: 'I agree that I didn't do the washing-up yesterday, but I have done everything else I'm supposed to.' If the criticism is untrue, say so. State your response: 'I disagree.' Then, add a positive comment about your behaviour in this respect: 'I'm very conscientious about doing my share.' Ask for an explanation: 'What makes you think I haven't been?'

You might find you want to probe a criticism a little further. In this case, you could ask for more feedback, saying, 'What is it about my behaviour that makes you think I'm selfish?', for example.

A result of tackling criticisms in this way is that genuine criticisms can be distinguished from manipulative put-downs. A genuine critic may give examples, meeting your assertive reply with an assertive response. A refusal to be specific or a backing-off probably indicates a lack of genuine concern.

If you are faced with an attitude like this, you could use a technique called 'fogging'. This helps you to play safe when you are being unfairly criticized or when you don't want to engage in a discussion of your 'fault' at that particular moment. What you do is calmly acknowledge that there may be some truth in what the speaker has said: 'You may be right; I suppose I may seem selfish to you sometimes.'

Note that you are neither agreeing nor disagreeing. You are not entering into the battle. You are not giving the other person the satisfaction of seeing you hurt or upset.

Exercise 60

Choose an issue of medium sensitivity from the list you made in the previous exercise. Imagine a likely future situation in which you are criticized about this. Using the above guidelines, decide on an appropriate response.

Situation: ....

....

What the other person is likely to say: ....

....

....

What I will say: ....

....

....

How I will say it: ....

....

....

Practise saying the words aloud, with accompanying assertive body language. Repeat the exercise with an issue that is highly sensitive.

Practise responding until you feel confident you can face the criticism and deal with it.

Exercise 61

It is possible that criticism from someone else may reinforce your own dissatisfaction with that aspect of your behaviour and strengthen your resolve to change it.

Look at the list you made in Exercise 58 (page 87). Taking steps to change one of the things you would like to be different will increase your feeling of being in control of your behaviour and will lessen stress-producing anxiety when your behaviour comes under critical scrutiny.

Choose one of the qualities that you marked with a C in the third column. Decide on three steps you can take to help you change the behaviour. Write them down below.

1 ....

2 ....

3 ....

Repeat this process for every behaviour you wrote a C by.

Now, decide in which order you will tackle these changes.

Give yourself a timescale and a way of knowing if your efforts have been successful. For example:

By next week, I will be more organized in the following ways:

1 ....

2 ....

3 ....

I will check to see if I have achieved these by doing the following:

....

....

....

Now do this for each of your planned changes.

By .... I will be more/less .... in the following ways:

1 ....

2 ....

3 ....

I will check to see if I have achieved these by doing the following:

....

....

....

Exercise 62

Coping effectively with criticism is a skill you can learn and one that will help you to face stressful interactions and emerge from them undiminished and, perhaps, strengthened by the encounter.

This also applies to situations where you have to choose whether or not to offer criticism to someone else. The need to confront people critically can be a severe source of stress, and many of us find it more difficult than being on the receiving end.

Think about critical comments and remarks you have made recently. List them below.

Comment   *To whom*

Using the above as a guide, answer the following questions.

	Yes	No
Do you criticize the person's behaviour rather than the person?	☐	☐
Do you say anything positive?	☐	☐
Do you acknowledge your own feelings?	☐	☐
Do you back down if the person attacks you in return?	☐	☐
Do you retract if challenged?	☐	☐
Do you apologize?	☐	☐
Do you speak critically in the heat of the moment?	☐	☐
Do you ever avoid giving criticism that you know is justified?	☐	☐

If you answered 'Yes' to the first three questions and 'No' to the rest, you are in the habit of giving *constructive* criticism. Being able to give criticism constructively and assertively makes it easier to deal with stressful situations and people and helps to build open and honest relationships.

Study sheet 11

Here are some guidelines for giving constructive criticism.

- Take the initiative and choose the time and place. It may also be a good idea to give the person some notice or warning.
- Be very clear in your mind about the specific behaviour you are criticizing. This will help you to focus on what you want to say and stop you generalizing.
- Be specific. Don't say, 'You're totally unreliable', but rather, 'The last three times I've asked you to post something for me you've either forgotten entirely or missed the post.'
- Comment on the *behaviour*, not the *person* (see above).
- Keep to the point. You may be very tempted to refer to other instances or to use the opportunity to unleash a load of built-up grievances, but don't! If you find you're about to use a phrase like, 'And another thing . . .' or 'And while we're on the subject of your behaviour at that party . . .', stop yourself! Keep in control of the point you are making.
- Acknowledge your feelings. If you have felt hurt or angry or frustrated as a result of the behaviour you are criticizing, say so.

- Acknowledge the other person's feelings/situation. Say 'I know you have been working to tight deadlines recently' or 'I realize what I am saying may be hurtful to you.'
- Ask for a specific, realistic change.
- Specify the positive and the negative consequences: 'If you do this, then. . . . If you don't, then . . .'.
- Ask for the other person's response. The response may be a criticism of you, in which case respond in the ways discussed in the last section. Remember, an assertive interaction is equal. The other person has the right, just as you have, to accept or reject criticism.
- Make clear what you have agreed.
- End on a positive note. In fact, a good model for offering constructive criticism is:

positive→negative→positive

In other words, begin by acknowledging something you value in the relationship with the other person, or some aspect of their behaviour you appreciate, then present the specific criticism, then finish with another positive statement.

Exercise 63

Choose two different situations in which you will have to criticize someone. Choose them from different areas of your life — one from home, perhaps, and one from work or outside your family. You might find it helpful to use an issue you have already raised, such as one from Exercise 50 (page 76), and work on presenting the criticism constructively.

Situation: ....

....

The person involved: ....

The behaviour I want to criticize: ....

....

What I will say: ....

....

....

Where I will say it: ....

When I will say it: ....

How I will say it: ....

....

....

Situation: ....

....

The person involved: ....

The behaviour I want to criticize: ....

....

What I will say: ....

....

....

Where I will say it: ....

When I will say it: ....

How I will say it: ....

....

....

If you find this has helped, practise saying the words aloud until you are satisfied that you sound calm and firm.

If you handle giving criticism well and constructively, you show respect for yourself and the other person. Giving direct, unaggressive and unmanipulative criticism shows you value them and your relationship and turns a potential source of stress into an opportunity for personal growth.

'I see red!'

Anger is a natural reaction we all experience and it can be the most destructive of all emotions. It can eat into the person who feels it and the people at whom it is directed. However, we can all learn to examine and evaluate the sources of our anger and to express it in a way that is healthy and reduces stress.

Scenario 14

Miles saw the radar gun a minute too late. He cursed and braked but he'd already driven into the speed trap. He was only going a little too fast. The unfairness of it filled him with rage and he fumed all the way home.

'I'm so angry!', he said as he burst through the front door. 'A little bit over — hardly a *dangerous* speed. What about all those people who race up the main road and never get pulled up?'

'You're not the only one who's angry,' said Fiona, 'I could have throttled Julia today. She took so long making up her mind where to eat that everywhere was full and even all the takeaway sandwiches were gone! I'm starving! And I was looking forward to a really nice lunch. I don't often get the chance.'

'I'll tell you what I'm looking forward to to now,' said Miles, 'a bit of peace and quiet.'

'Same here', agreed Fiona.

They had just settled down with their favourite Bach concerto playing gently in the background when a loud blast of heavy metal music came from next door. Miles leapt to his feet.

'Not again!' he yelled. 'It's intolerable! What right have they got to ruin our evening like this?'

He banged on the wall, outraged at this assault on their ears and their peace.

The anger that Miles and Fiona feel comes from their perception of the world. Miles' anger at the speed trap comes from his ideas about justice and injustice, what's right and wrong. He believes it's wrong that he should pay a penalty for a minor infringement of traffic law when other greater offenders go unpunished. His anger when the music blares from next door stems from the feeling that his space is being invaded and violated. Fiona's anger comes from frustration at not getting what she wanted and at experiencing discomfort and displeasure.

Exercise 64

What makes you angry? Make a list below of people, situations, things that irritate and annoy you. Begin with the minor things and build up to identifying major causes of anger for you.

Is there a common thread running through these examples?

You may be making yourself vulnerable to anger because of the way you perceive the world. Look at the beliefs inherent in the areas identified in Miles' and Fiona's world. Look at the beliefs inherent in the areas identified in Miles' and Fiona's experience and see if they are reflected in your list. Think about the following questions.

Violation of self

Do you invest too much of yourself in too many areas?
Do you strongly identify with and take pride in everything in your life? Such as:

family	friends	work	your hobby	sports team
home town	country	hero	political party	band.

If you over-identify with too many aspects, you are making yourself vulnerable on so many fronts that your anger is likely to be very easily triggered. If you take a great many things personally, you run the risk of being continually aroused but, in reality, your stress response is being activated to face what isn't really a threat. If you take criticism of your friend to include criticism of you or get very worked up about the team you support as if it were actually part of you, you are creating a heavy burden for yourself. The greater the number of areas that matter deeply to you, the greater the likely number of occasions on which your anger and defensiveness are easily aroused. Being aware of your tendency to this stress-producing characteristic should help you to reassess some of your attitudes and develop a more detached view in some areas of your life.[4]

As with all anger-inducing situations, try to differentiate between *degrees* of anger. Listen to your gut reaction and try to identify the strength of your feeling. Distinguish between feeling irritated, annoyed and furious. This can help you to gain a sense of perspective and to recognize how important or unimportant the situation is to you.

Frustration

If you have a low tolerance for frustration and discomfort, it is likely that you have an unrealistic view of the world. None of us has the right to get what we want and no one has the right never to experience discomfort, but 'This shouldn't happen to me' may characterize most of your thinking.

Injustice

If you are fired by a sense of unfairness, you are seeing the world as you *think* it should be, not as it *is*. Your moral judgements and sense of right and wrong are your own; when you try to impose them on others you are opening yourself to anger and stress.

Exercise 65

Take items from the list you made in the previous exercise that fit the above categories. For each one, give a short description of the situation and write beside it the kind of inner dialogue that will calm you and help you to see the situation differently. Here are a couple of examples.

Category: Violation of self.

Situation: Feeling angry when someone runs down my country.

Inner dialogue: My country isn't me. I can feel loyalty to it without totally identifying with it. I am not being personally attacked so I need not take this personally.

Category: Frustration.

Situation: Waiting for a train that is late.

Inner dialogue: I have to expect that the train will be late sometimes. This is one of those times. I have not been personally singled out to suffer this inconvenience.

Now, analyse items from your list in this way, repeating it as often as you like.

Category: ....

Situation: ....
....

Inner dialogue: ....
....
....

Anger is a result of how we perceive the world. It is caused by our failure to act intelligently by recognizing that our frustration is caused by the way we have chosen to define ourselves and, simply, by the very nature of life. Our beliefs that we can have everything — even achieve incompatible and mutually exclusive goals — and that we are entitled to what we want cause us stress and anxiety.

By looking at and changing your beliefs and attitudes, you can reduce the frequency and intensity of angry feelings and develop an approach to life that lessens your vulnerability to threat. If you practise the above exercise and the others you have worked through so far you will begin to alter your perception of situations and be able to choose not to see infringements of your personal rights and violations of your values as often as you do now.

However, anger is, of course, a justified and valid emotion. It is important to acknowledge it and express it appropriately. If anger is expressed at the right time to the right person, it can be healthy, productive and reduce stress. Repression of anger can lead to a range of psychological and physical disorders. When the stress response is triggered, it needs to be discharged; if we are constantly in a state of arousal with no outlet we make ourselves vulnerable to the kinds of illness described in Chapter 1. Expressing anger assertively, therefore, is an important skill and one that can be learned.

Exercise 66

How do you deal with your anger? Answering the following questions will help you assess your way of managing angry feelings.

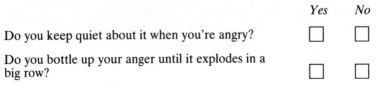

	Yes	No
Do you keep quiet about it when you're angry?	☐	☐
Do you bottle up your anger until it explodes in a big row?	☐	☐

Do you appear hurt when, in fact, you are angry? ☐ ☐

Do you express your anger to the person or people
involved? ☐ ☐

Do you take it out on someone or something else? ☐ ☐

It may be that you find it difficult to express your anger openly and
honestly. This could be because of some of the messages you have
inherited. Put a tick by any of the following beliefs that reflect your own
ideas about anger.

☐ Anger isn't 'nice'.

☐ Other people will be upset if I show anger.

☐ People won't like me if I lose my temper.

☐ If I hide it, it will go away.

☐ If I pretend it's all right it *will* be all right.

☐ My parents never expressed anger in front of me.

☐ 'Temper tantrums' were punished in our house.

☐ It's more acceptable to cry or sulk than it is to be angry.

If you ticked several of these statements, it is likely that your inability to
acknowledge and express your anger is creating stress for yourself and for
those around you. You may be restricting your own growth and the
development of healthy relationships with people close to you.

Study sheet 12

Here are some guidelines for managing your own anger.

- Recognize and acknowledge that you are angry. Claim the feeling with
  a statement beginning with 'I' — 'I feel very annoyed/angry/irritated'.
  Avoid phrases like 'You make me feel . . .' or 'It makes me mad when
  you . . .'. Take responsibility for your anger. There is no need to feel
  ashamed of it.
- Test the level of your anger. Listen to your gut reaction. Feel the
  difference between a minor irritation and something deeper. This will
  help you to assess how to deal with it.
- If you are too angry to deal with the person or the situation at the
  moment, take some time out. Walk away or say you will discuss it later.
  Discharge your feelings by doing something physical, like walking or

digging the garden or shouting or hitting a cushion. When you are ready, express your feelings differently.

- Share your feelings. The action of expressing them will help you to control them.
- Decide what you will do once you have acknowledged, understood and expressed your feelings. Will you let go of the feeling of anger and allow the relationship to move on, free from guilt or recrimination and strengthened by the honest disclosure of feelings?

Dealing with other people's anger can be a stressful experience. However, if you apply the same principles you learned for dealing with criticism (given in Study sheet 10, page 89) as a basis, you should be able to cope with these situations more effectively. Here are some guidelines for dealing with other people's anger.

- Remember, you are not responsible for someone else's anger.
- You have the right to walk away from anyone who is shouting at you.
- Acknowledge the other person's feelings. This will help to diffuse their anger; ignoring it will make it worse. Say something like, 'I can see you're very angry about this.'
- Acknowledge your own feelings. If you feel angry in response or upset, say so. If you feel you cannot discuss the matter at the moment because of these feelings, say so.
- When it is appropriate, apply the guidelines offered in Study sheet 10.
- An expression of anger, an outburst, a row, a heated discussion — these will change a relationship. Decide what you will do now. Will you discuss the matter again, in a calmer context? Will you acknowledge what happened, without trying to sweep it under the carpet and pretend nothing was said? Will you enable the relationship to accommodate the anger and move on, with both of you having learned from the experience?

4

Changing your lifestyle

'There aren't enough hours in the day'

Scenario 15

The phone rang as Martha was dashing out of the house. For a second she hovered, wondering whether she should just let it ring — she was already running late. She picked up the receiver.

'I'm glad I caught you,' said her mother, 'what time am I picking up the children this afternoon? You didn't say.'

'Oh,' said Martha, 'hang on a minute.' She rummaged through a drawer stuffed with letters, bills, cards and bits cut out of magazines looking for the notices about Kirsty's netball tournament and Alex's swimming gala. She came across an invitation she had meant to reply to last week and put it behind the plant pot to remind her. At last she found the relevant bits of paper. She read out the times and places to her mother and waited as she wrote them down. She was now well and truly late for meeting Jenny.

'Never mind,' said Jenny, 'we've still got plenty of time. What do you want to do first?'

'I'm not sure — perhaps look for Ann's wedding present?'

'Fine. Have you brought the list with you?'

Martha searched her bag. 'I don't think so. I can't remember what I did with it. I can remember most of it, though.'

Jenny waited patiently by the counter as Martha tried to decide if the terracotta Ann had specified was for towels or sheets. 'I'll have to leave it', she said in the end. 'I'll have to dash back when I've got the list. Shall we look for your outfit?'

'OK,' said Jenny, 'the most likely place is that shop at the top of town.'

As they neared the shop, Martha said, 'I need to pick up some dry-cleaning and the shop closes early today.'

They retraced their steps to the dry-cleaners at the end of town they had just left, but halfway there Martha said, 'No, tell you what, I won't bother to pick it up. I don't want to carry it around all afternoon.' They walked back up the hill.

As they ate their lunch with the carrier bag containing Jenny's new outfit safely stowed under the table, Jenny asked, 'How are the job applications going?'

Martha grimaced, 'There's not much around, but Taylors were advertising last week. I had meant to send off an application last night, but then I had to sew on Alex's swimming badges for the gala today, and then Penny dropped by, so I didn't get round to it. I'll do it tonight if there's time.'

When Martha got home, her mother was waiting to go. 'Oh, can't you stay for a bit?', asked Martha. She'd been looking forward to a chat about the wedding arrangements.

'No, I told you I'd have to be off promptly. I'm playing bridge tonight.'

'There never seems to be any time to talk these days', said Martha wistfully. 'I don't know where the days go. I just seem to dash from pillar to post achieving nothing. No wonder I'm always worn out.'

Martha's life is stressful because she doesn't organize her time efficiently. Because she doesn't plan how she will use her time, she wastes this valuable resource. She doesn't plan ahead so that she is prepared; she is disorganized and has no system for dealing with the household paperwork so she always has to search and rummage for what she wants, and often finds items too late. She doesn't have a clear sense of priorities to enable her to plan, so she sews on badges at the last minute instead of dealing with her job application, which is a more urgent task. She allows herself to be distracted by Penny's visit. Talking with her mother is important to her, but this activity is edged out by other demands that matter less to her.

Martha has as much time as everyone else. Some people, however, use their time more efficiently, flexibly and creatively.

Much stress stems from our failure to organize our lives effectively. Without effective organization and planning, we respond to outside pressures as they occur and often find that they pile up so that life becomes a series of crises, and we spend all our time dealing with them. Coping with these events leaves us no time to do the things we want to do, so we feel frustrated and demoralized, which compounds the stressful experience.

Planning and assessing how you want to use your time not only protects you from stress, it also enables you to recognize and achieve your personal goals and to enjoy the satisfaction that comes with this.

Exercise 67

How do you use your time? List all the activities you engage in in one day, including sleeping, eating, shopping, watching television, and so on, in the order in which they occur. Be as precise as you can, whether you are listing things you did at home or at work — for example, 10–10.30, read report; 10.30–10.45, chatted to June at the coffee machine.

Time   *Activity*

7.00 _____

7.30 _____

8.00 _____

8.30 _____

9.00 _____

9.30 _____

10.00 _____

10.30 _____

11.00 _____

11.30 _____

12.00 _____

12.30 _____

1.00 _____

1.30 _____

2.00 _____

2.30 _____

3.00 _____

3.30 _____

4.00 _____

4.30 _____

5.00 _____

5.30 _____

6.00 _____

6.30 _____

7.00 _____

7.30 _____

8.00 _____

8.30 _____

9.00 _____

9.30 _____

10.00 _____

10.30 _____

11.00 _____

Exercise 68

Add up how much time you spent on each of the activities you listed in the previous exercise. List the activities below with the time beside it. Leave the third column blank for now.

Activity	Time spent	Satisfaction/enjoyment
....		1☐ 2☐ 3☐ 4☐ 5☐
....		1☐ 2☐ 3☐ 4☐ 5☐
....		1☐ 2☐ 3☐ 4☐ 5☐
....		1☐ 2☐ 3☐ 4☐ 5☐
....		1☐ 2☐ 3☐ 4☐ 5☐
....		1☐ 2☐ 3☐ 4☐ 5☐
....		1☐ 2☐ 3☐ 4☐ 5☐
....		1☐ 2☐ 3☐ 4☐ 5☐
....		1☐ 2☐ 3☐ 4☐ 5☐
....		1☐ 2☐ 3☐ 4☐ 5☐

Next, for each activity, tick the number in the third column that indicates how much satisfaction/enjoyment you got from each one (one being low, five high).

You may well find that you are spending too much of your available time on activities that are not particularly satisfying. This could be because you have not identified and planned time for what you really want.

Study sheet 13

Time management is not about making time to fill your day with more activities. Indeed, viewing time in terms of quantity rather than quality will only make your life more stressful. We can create stress for ourselves by feeling unable to do all the things we 'have' to do *and* by doing things that are irrelevant or unsatisfying. Some aspects of time management are to do with adding up time in terms of figures and percentages, but its basis is deeper than that. It is a way of enabling you to exercise choice over how you spend this most valuable resource, time, in order to manage the pressures and demands placed on you in such a way that you maintain the balance and sense of purpose that will enhance your life.

A vital first step is becoming clear about your own goals and what motivates you. You will then be able to decide how to use your time to advance the achievement of these goals and also be able to identify what prevents you from using your time in this constructive way.

The four simple steps to successful time management are:

1 establish goals
2 prioritize
3 plan
4 organize.

Exercise 69

Achieving personal goals brings high self-esteem and satisfaction. Being aware of them and working towards them brings a sense of direction and purpose to our daily lives.

Goal planning is about deciding what you really want to do and working out a way of doing it.

Write down a list of what you would like to accomplish in your lifetime. Include material things, personal ambitions, relationships, lifestyle . . . making it as long or as short as you like.

This should give you an overall picture.

Now, break the picture down, focusing on which areas of your life these relate to. Although they can overlap, it is a useful way of helping you to see your goals clearly.

Work   *Personal*   *Social*

Now, go through and eliminate any goals that are completely unattainable. Some pipe dreams, like playing in the World Cup, may have to remain pleasant fantasies.

Make sure each goal is clear and specific. General comments about earning more money or taking up new interests are not as helpful as specific aims, such as 'Be able to speak French when we have our holiday there next year'.

Look for inconsistencies. For instance, it may not be possible to have children *and* an immaculate home.

Now rank your goals in order of their importance to you.

Exercise 70

Having established your goals, the next step is to break them down into objectives. This means that you split up your goals into manageable pieces and state a specific aim that will take you along the road to achieving it. For example, if one of your goals is to play a major role in local politics, an

110

objective might be, 'Join the local branch of my party and attend at least one meeting a month'.

It is useful to give your objectives a timescale, too — achieve it within a month, in six months' time, by the end of the year or whatever.

Write your goals and objectives down below.

Goal   *Objective*

Now, break down your objectives into specific activities. For each one, write a list of things you can do to enable you to fulfil it. For example, your objective of joining your local political party may be put in motion by making a phone call to the branch secretary.

Goal   *Objective*   *Action*

Once you have established your goals and related activities, the question of managing your time effectively has a specific focus. Learning to set your priorities and stick to them is a vital step in enabling you to deal with the many, various and conflicting demands that daily life throws at you. Being clear about what is the best use of your time, the highest priority at any particular moment, means you have a powerful tool to help you cope with pressure.

Exercise 71

Every day, list everything you need to do. Don't bother to include routine matters that will get done as a matter of course, but make a note of all the other things. You may like to group them and you can do this in any way you find useful — perhaps by putting together all similar activities, like phone calls to be made or people to be seen, or you may prefer to group tasks by location, such as, things to do at home, at work, in town, and so on.

List the things to be done today or tomorrow.

Check to make sure that you have included tasks to do with the goals you have identified. Look at your goal, objective and action list made in the previous exercise and be certain to build these into your list.

Look through your list and see if there are any tasks you can *delegate*. Don't do anything yourself that someone else can do. Don't just think of delegation in terms of subordinates at work, think of all the people you live and work with who may be able to do certain tasks more quickly, easily or even with more enjoyment than you. Give other people things that don't require your personal involvement.

All tasks that must be done at once, mark with an A. Any that would be best done today, mark with a B. Any that can wait, or it would be nice to do, mark with a C. Include items to do with your personal goals in the A category. If you don't, they will remain things it would be nice to do one day when you have time. You *do* have time — use it.

Re-write your list below, ordering the entries by these categories.

A   *B*   *C*

You now have a helpful 'To do' list. This is a fundamental time management tool, your at-a-glance guide to the best way to use your time.

Study sheet 14

To be effective, the list must be *used* effectively!

The As are the most important. Do them before the Bs and Cs, even if they are less attractive. These are the tasks that you want to achieve. Some of them may be difficult things that require your full concentration. If so, plan to do them when you are feeling your best. If you are not sure when this is, monitor your concentration and tiredness levels for a few days. If you are always awake early and buzzing with energy, do some of your A work then. If you know you feel sleepy at a certain time, try to use this time for something else — a less demanding A task or an element of an A task that is the least taxing or use the time for a B or C task.

Examine your C tasks. Would it really matter if they *weren't* done? Ask yourself what is the worst thing that could happen if you eliminated that item altogether. Do you tend to do lots of C items at the expense of the more important As? If you do, remind yourself of the 80/20 rule.

This is an idea that was developed in the nineteenth century by an Italian economist and sociologist called Vilfredo Pareto. His principle states that 80 per cent of results comes from 20 per cent of items. So, in a list of ten items, doing two of them will get you the best results. Find these two on your list. Make sure they are on the A list, and do them now. It doesn't matter if the other eight don't get done — concentrate on the ones that will help you achieve your goals.

Keep reminding yourself not to get overwhelmed by or bogged down with low-value activities; concentrate on the ones that really matter.

Don't procrastinate. Procrastination is closely linked with stress. Avoiding doing tasks we set ourselves ultimately leads to more pressure. Recognize the early warning signs — tidying the desk before you start anything, sharpening all the pencils you can find, rearranging the items on the noticeboard, straightening the magazines . . . We all have our favourite ways of putting off doing something! You will feel better, though, if you do it now. Reward yourself for getting it done. If you've written that difficult letter, spend ten minutes browsing through a magazine or have a cup of coffee.

Promise yourself something when you've completed a task. Use these positive reinforcements to encourage yourself and keep up the momentum.

Keep your list updated. Cross off each item as it's done and add things as they occur to you. Re-write the list at the end of the day.

Priorities will change. Some B items may become A items, for example, or they may become less important than you thought and go on the C list. Some things may drop off the list altogether as you realize that they don't have to be done.

It is important to keep up the A items. They are the key to your personal achievement. If you find there are only Bs and Cs on your list at any point, review your goals and objectives. Take the opportunity to use time for one of your A activities.

Allow more time than you think you'll need.

Leave some time unscheduled. Don't try to fill up every minute with a planned activity — leave some space for emergencies and the unexpected.

Plan each week according to these principles and make a fresh 'To do' list every day.

Exercise 72

Good organization is the key to managing your tasks efficiently. It is highly likely that you can pinpoint areas where more careful organization would relieve some of the pressure in your life and enable you to make better use of your time. One aspect of our lives that can cause distress and frustration is the amount of paperwork we face every day. Assess how you cope with it using the following check-list.

	Yes	No
Do you use a calendar/appointment diary?	☐	☐
Is your desk/workspace cluttered?	☐	☐
Do you have a filing system for papers at home?	☐	☐
Do you sort papers according to A/B/C priority?	☐	☐
Does paper pile up as you decide what to do with it?	☐	☐
Do you regularly throw paper away?	☐	☐
Do you ever put letters and so on somewhere 'for now'?	☐	☐
Do you have to shuffle through papers to find what you want?	☐	☐
Do you ever keep papers 'just in case'?	☐	☐

If you answered 'Yes' to the first, third, fourth and sixth questions and 'No' to the others, you are handling your paperwork well.

Study sheet 15

Here are some guidelines for dealing with paperwork.

- Divide papers, incoming letters and so on into three piles according to A/B/C priority.
- Handle each piece of paper once.
- Decide if it is:
    — to be acted on by you — if so, do it
    — to be dealt with by someone else — if so, delegate
    — to be memorized by you — if so note it and throw it away
    — to be studied later — if so, file it
    — not within your sphere of interest/responsibility — if so, throw it away.
  Limit your choice to the three 'Ds': Do, delegate, dump.

- Devise a filing/sorting system for personal and domestic paperwork.
- Keep papers in a specific location.
- Ask yourself, 'What would happen if I threw this piece of paper away?' Assess its importance by your answer.
- Keep your workspaces uncluttered.

Make time your ally, not your enemy. By employing the three steps of goal setting — prioritizing, planning and organizing — you can make your environment and your daily life less stressful. Managing your time effectively means you are taking control of your life and directing your energies into productive areas. The challenge of making time work for you can be positive and stimulating.

Couch potatoes

Physical exercise is of enormous benefit in dealing with stress. It helps to discharge the energy that is stored up in the body because our systems are responding to stressors but have no outlet for action and it staves off the effects of every day wear and tear by keeping joints flexible and supple. Not only does it improve our physical well-being, it also protects us from the kind of mental fatigue that often accompanies stress and pressure. Physical fitness provides great protection against stress and stress-related illnesses, strengthening our resources to cope with all levels of pressure.

Scenario 16

Dean chatted to Terry as they waited for the lift. 'The parking situation's really out of control', he said. 'Do you know, I had to leave my car in the next street and walk all the way here!'

Terry grimaced in sympathy. 'Too bad', he said. 'I wish this lift would get a move on.'

'I sometimes think it would be quicker to take the stairs', said Dean.

They got out at the second floor and went to their respective offices. 'I'll give you a call at lunchtime, then', said Dean.

He settled down to work at his VDU and worked steadily until the refreshment trolley came round.

'Your usual?' asked Frieda.

'Thanks', said Dean, balancing the coffee and doughnut on the side of his desk. He carried on working until it was time to ring Terry and see if he was ready for lunch.

They took the lift down to the canteen, where they sat in the corner and chatted about the Test Match as they tucked into shepherd's pie. 'Better get back then', said Dean as the clock crept round.

Dean worked steadily until the end of the day then walked the few paces from the office to the lift. He felt a pang of annoyance at having to walk a little to collect the car. He drove home and put the car in the garage; they were going to the pictures that evening, but they'd use Dawn's car.

They were lucky with the parking that evening, being early enough to get a space right outside the cinema. They both enjoyed the film and told Ken about it in the pub when they popped in for a drink on the way home.

Dean yawned as he unlocked the front door. 'I'm ready for bed,' he said, 'I'm exhausted — I've been on the go all day!'

Dean would probably not think of himself as a couch potato. He works hard at his job and doesn't just flop in front of the television every evening. He goes to the cinema, to the pub and to see friends. He may describe his life as full and active, but in fact, he engages in very little physical activity. He drives everywhere, usually door to door, and feels a little put out if he has to walk a short distance. At work he uses the lift when possible and moves from his desk only at lunchtime. He doesn't even have to move to get a cup of coffee and he communicates with colleagues from his desk or on the phone. His lifestyle includes practically no exercise.

Dean isn't under severe pressure. He is not aware of any stress in his life. But, by neglecting his physical fitness, he is unwittingly making himself vulnerable to stress and stress-related illnesses and weakening his ability to cope with pressure.

Exercise 73

What is your attitude to exercise?

	Yes	No
I enjoy exercise.	☐	☐
I find exercise boring.	☐	☐
I have to force myself to exercise.	☐	☐
I feel good when I exercise.	☐	☐
I find it hard to fit in regular exercise.	☐	☐
Exercise is part of my life.	☐	☐
There is no point to exercise unless it is competitive.	☐	☐
I enjoy exercising with someone else.	☐	☐
I exercise now and then.	☐	☐

I look forward to exercise. □ □

If you answered 'Yes' to the first, fourth, sixth and tenth questions, you probably see exercise in a positive light and are prepared to look at your exercise pattern and adjust it, if necessary, to make it even more effective in stress-proofing your life.

If you answered 'Yes' to the fifth, eighth and ninth questions, it is likely that you recognize the benefits of exercise, particularly if it has a social dimension, but are not motivated to maintain a regular pattern.

If you answered 'Yes' to the second and third questions, you obviously dislike exercise and could look at ways of building it into your life in an acceptable way.

If you answered 'Yes' to the seventh question, you may wish to reassess this attitude and try a different approach. See the last paragraph of the following study sheet.

Study sheet 16

Why exercise, then?

The fitter you are, the less likely you are to develop physical and mental disorders. If you are fit, you have more energy to deal with daily problems and more resilience to meet setbacks and pressure. People who take regular, controlled exercise have the resources to avoid stress-related illnesses such as heart attacks and strokes. They become ill less frequently, recover more quickly and are more able to cope with tasks requiring mental ability.

The physical benefits of exercise are many. Short periods of regular exercise — 20 minutes three times a week — can improve the function of the heart, muscles and circulatory system. It makes the heart pump efficiently, which releases more oxygen into the bloodstream and reduces blood pressure and blood sugar levels. It helps to strengthen the joints and muscles and to maintain flexibility.

Regular exercise counteracts the effects of the body's automatic stress response. It allows discharge of energy, whether through a 'hard-hitting' sport like squash or a rhythmical one like walking or dancing. It can reduce your anxiety level by speeding up the rate at which lactic acid, which is caused by shallow breathing and creates feelings of mental and physical exhaustion, is oxidized and removed from your circulation.

Lack of exercise is itself a stressor. If you don't use your body, it won't function at optimum level. Even if you are basically healthy, you are subject to physical deterioration if you take no exercise at all. Muscles become weak and hormone levels decrease until you begin to feel tired all the time. If you don't exercise, your body becomes incapable of dealing with the kind of extra pressure that we all have to face from time to time.

There are psychological benefits of exercise as well. Exercise releases endorphins, which are mood-elevating proteins with a similar chemical structure to opium and morphine. These are sometimes known as 'happy hormones' because of the feelings of well-being they generate. They also help to calm the body and allow it to function under stress. As an example, they appear after about two kilometres' running, or the equivalent. As well as this, you experience a boost of adrenalin immediately after exercising that adds to your feeling of well-being.

Exercise can also give you a psychological boost by increasing your self-esteem. Not only do you *feel* better when you exercise, you *look* better as well. When your circulation is stimulated and muscle tension reduced, the blood flows more freely to the skin's surface and makes your skin look clearer and healthier. Other benefits are better, more confident posture and bearing.

So, now we know exercise has so many benefits, what exercise should we do?

Consider two factors here: choose the kind of exercise you enjoy and can do regularly and the kind of activity that will have the greatest physical and psychological benefits for you personally.

You need to choose an activity or balance of activities in which you can engage three times a week for a minimum of 20 minutes. Shorter periods of time don't allow the body to change sufficiently and you may find you expend time and energy without achieving a basic level of fitness.

Think about the three main ways in which exercise affects your body. It provides:

- strength
- suppleness
- stamina.

Activities such as jogging, weightlifting and cycling strengthen the cardio-vascular system. Suppleness and strength are developed through activities such as aerobics. If your favourite form of exercise is one that focuses on suppleness and flexibility, such as yoga or certain workout programmes, it might be a good idea also to take up an activity that improves your stamina.

Stamina is the key element that will help you cope with pressure. Activities such as swimming, cycling, jogging and fast walking improve your heart and lung capacity, build up your endurance and help your body to work at a higher metabolic rate for prolonged periods.

Other activities that will enable you to maintain basic fitness, if undertaken regularly and for the minimum suggested time, include judo, rowing, squash (although you should actually do back-up vigorous exercise to enable your body to withstand the demands squash makes on it), swimming, fencing, gymnastics and so on.

119

If your favourite physical activity is badminton, cricket, horse-riding, archery, table tennis, gentle walking, golf or billiards, you should try to top up your exercise with other activities to maintain a good fitness level or simply increase the time spent undertaking the gentler activity.

If you answered 'Yes' to the seventh question on the check-list in the previous exercise, you may be adding to pressure in your life. If a preoccupation with winning is a key element in your exercise programme, you are probably increasing your level of tension and anxiety. You could think about finding some other form of activity or work on seeing squash, golf, tennis or whatever as just a game that is played for exercise and enjoyment. Try to see winning as a nice bonus, not as the main objective.

Exercise 74

Review your present rate of physical activity. Bearing in mind the criteria that exercise should be:

- enjoyable
- regular
- controlled
- increase stamina.

Work out a programme that will increase your present level of fitness. If you take no exercise at the moment, think about ways of gently building up your fitness.

If you are already fit, think about ways of maintaining your good level of fitness and of increasing your stamina.

I could become fit by ....

....

I could become more fit by ....

....

....

I could maintain my good level of fitness by ....

....

....

My best time for exercise is ....

....

I exercise best . . . (by myself, with someone else, or other) ....

....

If this programme doesn't work, if you don't enjoy what you try, change it. Exercise is for you and although, of course, some discipline and commitment is necessary if you are to stick to a programme, there is no point in grinding on with something you dislike. Make exercise an integral part of your life and an enjoyable strategy for strengthening your resources and combating stress.

'I feel so wound up'

Exercise 75

Check to see if you are doing any of the following now:

- clenching your teeth
- frowning
- hunching your shoulders
- tapping your foot
- clenching your fists
- holding your stomach tightly
- clenching your toes
- biting your fingernails
- twiddling with your hair.

Now look at yourself in a mirror and answer the following questions.

- Is one shoulder higher than the other?
- Is your neck thrust forward?
- Are your knees tightly locked?
- Is your back tense and rigid?

If you were not aware that your body exhibits any of these signs of tension you may be so wound up all the time that you either just accept these reactions or, maybe, don't even notice them. They may have become second nature, so that you accept tight and tense muscles almost as a natural and inevitable physical state.

Relaxation is a known antidote to stress. If your mind and body are relaxed, it is impossible to be in a state of tension and anxiety. What many of us don't realize is that being relaxed is not the same as just doing nothing, but rather is a very positive and specific mode and one we can learn to adopt at will. Conscious relaxing is an essential part of dealing with stress and pressure and, like the other strategies we have been exploring, it can be learned.

Having learned to relax, you will feel its advantages immediately. You will become aware of the areas of your body that are stiff and tense and will be able to experience almost instant relief from this tension. Relaxation exercises can bring your whole body from a state of tension to one of relaxation in one minute. Five minutes' relaxation work on your face, neck and shoulder muscles can get rid of a headache and 20 to 30 minutes' work can bring about deep relaxation of body and mind so that you move from a state of tension to a state of enhanced mental and physical energy.

Relaxation exercises are an invaluable strategy to help you deal with pressure. Learning some simple techniques will enable you to combat fatigue and improve concentration by restoring balance to your central nervous system. You will sleep better and your digestive system will work more effectively.

Study sheet 17

When we are relaxed, changes take place in our bodies that are the reverse of those which take place when we react to stress. This is because a different side of the autonomic nervous system is being activated.

The 'fight or flight' response is triggered by the *sympathetic* side of the nervous system. This is the one that raises your arousal level in the ways we looked at in Chapter 1. The other side of the nervous system is called the *parasympathetic* side, and this reverses the effect of the sympathetic side. The parasympathetic side lowers arousal to calm you down. It comes into play to return your heart and breathing to their previous level, to send the blood back to your digestive system and to lower your blood pressure.

If you are under constant pressure, the sympathetic side is constantly activated. This means that the parasympathetic side is dormant and could be underused for long periods of time. Relaxation exercises and techniques can help you to reactivate it. By relaxing muscles and releasing tension, we can cancel the 'alert' signals that are sent to and from the brain and can tap into our body's resources to make full use of them in meeting stressful demands and in improving the quality of life.

The following four types of exercise — breathing, tensing/relaxing, progressive muscle relaxation, and imaging — are basic relaxation techniques you can practise until you are able to move into a state of relaxation very quickly whenever you realize that it is necessary.

Exercise 76

Are you breathing properly? Place your right hand on your upper abdomen, just above your navel, and your left in the middle of your upper chest. If you are breathing correctly, your right hand should move as you breathe, and your left hand remain still.

Breathing properly is an excellent way to reduce tension and anxiety. Breathing in supplies the body with oxygen and breathing out gets rid of carbon dioxide and other waste products. Using your full breathing potential ensures the optimum flow of oxygen and the complete elimination of harmful wastes.

The following breathing exercise can be done in ten seconds, no matter where you are. It is particularly helpful in moments of stress, but it is also useful to do this at regular intervals throughout the day, perhaps at the beginning of a task and then when you have finished it.

1 Take a deep, slow breath in and hold it for five seconds. Feel your abdomen expand as you do this.
2 Breathe out slowly, to a count of five. Concentrate on expelling *all* the air in your lungs to create a vacuum that will refill as a reflex action. If you're alone, you could make a noise like 'whoo' as you do this to help you feel the air being let out. Keep the outbreath going for as long as you can. Keep it relaxed for a few seconds before you inhale again.
3 Breathe in again. Make every breath slow and steady and exactly the same as the one before it and the one after it.

Exercise 77

This exercise uses the technique of alternately tensing and relaxing groups of muscles to relax them — an idea originally developed by Dr Edmund Jacobson in the 1930s. His research made him aware of the close connection between tense muscles and tense feelings, and he found a way of helping his patients totally relax the body as an aid to total relaxation of the mind. His method was very involved — requiring about 60 hours of training to master — but later practitioners have used abbreviated forms of it. You should find a marked improvement in your ability to relax if you practise this exercise for a few weeks. You should be able to trigger the relaxation response whenever you feel tense or anxious and should find that relaxing becomes natural and spontaneous. This is what you do.

1 Wear loose, comfortable clothing.
2 Lie on your back or sit on a chair that supports your back.

3 Start with your head. Think about your head. Raise your eyebrows as high as you can or frown fiercely. Tense. Hold the position for about five seconds. Relax — immediately, not gradually. Let the tension go, let the creases and wrinkles drop away. Focus on the difference between tension and relaxation.

4 Think about your jaw. Clench it tight. Clench your teeth. Tense. Hold the position for about five seconds. Relax, letting your jaw drop and hang loose. Note the difference.

5 Think about your neck. Drop your chin to your chest with the muscles at the front and, at the same time, pull your head back with the muscles in the back of your neck. Tense. Hold the position for about five seconds. Relax. Let your head roll loosely and heavily.

6 Think about your left hand and arm. Clench your hand tightly and feel the tension in the fist. Tense. Hold the position for about five seconds. Relax. Let the tension flow from your arm. Feel your fingers uncurl and dangle loosely and heavily.

7 Think about your right hand and arm. Tense and relax as for your left hand and arm.

8 Think about your left leg, calf and thigh. Push down hard with your thigh muscles, bending your toes as well. Tense. Hold the position for about five seconds. Relax. Feel the tension drain away as your leg, foot and toes go limp and heavy.

9 Think about your right leg, calf and thigh. Repeat 8.

10 Try to practise this technique once a day for several weeks. Become aware of the different states of tension and relaxation.

Once you become aware of tension in your muscles, you can train yourself to activate the relaxation response very quickly. You could work on being able to do this without actually tensing the muscles first but by remembering and reproducing the feeling of letting the tension drain away.

Exercise 78

If your mind and body are relaxed, you automatically exclude the tension that makes your muscles tight. Practising this basic technique for relaxing your muscles will enable you to cope with your emotional and bodily reactions in stress situations as well as producing the kind of relaxed state that is one of your most effective answers to stressful demands. In the following exercise, you reach a state of deep relaxation by using your imagination and giving your body instructions about how it is feeling.

1 Lie or sit somewhere with the whole of your body supported. Make yourself totally comfortable.

2 Tell yourself you are beginning to feel relaxed — 'I am feeling heavier and heavier. My breathing is slow and deep, deep and slow . . .'
3 Begin with either the top or bottom of your body, saying to yourself 'My feet are/head is getting heavy. My toes are/head is floppy and relaxed.' Repeat. Use your imagination to make the heaviness creep into your muscles.
4 Move slowly through every muscle group, instructing the muscles of each to relax at a deeper and deeper level.
5 When your body is completely relaxed and heavy, lie still and concentrate on slow, rhythmic breathing.

Make your own relaxation tape to do this exercise to. You can use the phrases given above as they are or alter them in any way that helps you. Then, write the script in which you tell yourself what to do step by step. You can continue or prolong the steps above as much as you like. Then, record it yourself or get someone whose voice you find relaxing to record it for you. You could add soothing, relaxing music if you wish. Keep in mind that you are evoking a pattern of gradual relaxation throughout your body.

Exercise 79

Creative imaging or visualization has enormous potential in helping you to achieve a deeply relaxed state. Its basis is the use of mental images associated with peace, beauty, calm and tranquillity. When you conjure up these images in a deliberate and systematic way, your mind sends messages to the rest of your body, telling it to relax. The brain begins to associate certain mental images with relaxation so that the relaxation state can be easily reached. This is an ancient technique that can be used to counteract nervousness and tension and help to overcome fear and apprehension. The use of positive imagery to combat negative thoughts is effective and enjoyable.

The exercise that follows uses imagery of sand and sun as an aid to relaxation, but this is just one of many possible images, so feel free to use any mental picture that works for you personally. If you have bad memories of a beach holiday, then obviously this example isn't right for you! Let your mind drift through pleasant memories; follow the thoughts that intrude or stray pictures that appear. Your own memories are likely to be fresh and vivid and work well for you. Pictures many people find helpful involve the sea, water, exotic islands, the countryside, woods and forests. . . .

1 Find a quiet room where you will not be disturbed.
2 Lie on your back and close your eyes.

3 Concentrate on breathing slowly and rhythmically.
4 Imagine yourself lying on a beach on a warm, sunny day. Imagine your muscles loose and heavy as they sink into the golden sand. Feel its softness lie heavily and soothingly on your muscles as they sink into its golden warmth. Feel yourself becoming more and more relaxed as your limbs and muscles become loose and limp. The sun's rays surround you with their warmth. Feel them penetrating every part of your body, warming it within and without. Imagine the physical sensations of this — become part of the scene. Feel your muscles relax and dissolve as your body sinks into total peace and relaxation. Tell yourself, 'I feel warm and relaxed. The sun is warming me through and through.' Repeat these phrases gently and rhythmically.
5 Continue the exercise for about 20 minutes, then gradually come round. Open your eyes, breathe deeply and stretch.

This and the previous three exercises you have just practised are vital tools for stress management. Relaxation is a known cure for stress, so make it a state you can acquire quickly and at will. Your inner mind can produce a relaxation so that you can trigger the 'relaxation response' rather than the 'stress response'. The relaxation response is just as natural, but it is positive and beneficial and, with practise, easily attainable.

Comfort food

We are constantly receiving advice about healthy eating and the physical damage we are inflicting on ourselves if we ignore it. What you may not realize is the effect diet has on our ability to cope with stress. Someone eating a healthy diet is much more able to withstand the physical effects of stress and much less likely to suffer from stress-related illnesses than someone whose diet is lacking in the essential elements. Paying attention to what we eat is one of the most positive steps we can take to protect our bodies from the harmful effects of stress and to increase our stress-resistance.

Scenario 17

Trisha hurried downstairs and grabbed her coat. 'Are you ready, kids?' It was her day for the school run and she'd overslept. No time for breakfast. She'd have something when she got back. She strapped the baby into his seat and the other two piled into theirs.

When she returned, much later than she'd expected because of a burst water main on the main road, she was starving and her eyes were pricking with tiredness. Harry had been restless most of the night and she'd had to go to him several times. She'd got up early to see Jim off on his business trip and was just drifting back to sleep when the alarm went off. No wonder she'd dropped off again. She put the kettle on to boil and popped some bread in the toaster. Reading the paper and washing down thick slices of toast and marmalade with heavily sugared tea, she began to feel her spirits and her energy level rising.

She and Kerry had planned to take the toddlers to the park. On the way to Kerry's, Trisha picked up a couple of apple doughnuts. 'Lovely,' said Kerry, 'I'll make some proper coffee, shall I? I imagine we could both do with it nice and strong!'

At lunchtime, they did the children fish fingers and baked beans. 'I'm not hungry, though,' said Trisha, 'I'll be eating this evening with the children, anyway.' They just had tea and biscuits as they supervised the children's meal.

At the park, Trisha felt a bit faint as she bent down to pick up Harry and put him on the slide. 'I expect it's the heat', said Kerry.

'I wish I'd had some lunch after all,' said Trisha, 'let's go over to the café.' She picked up a can of coke and a bar of chocolate. 'That's better — I'm fine now.'

Trisha cooked pasta for the children in the evening, but didn't really feel like eating any herself. She had a lot to do and didn't want to sit down for long. When she'd finished all her tasks and Harry was asleep and the others busy doing homework, she made herself a bacon sandwich and a cup of coffee. As she was eating it, Jim phoned to say he'd arrived and to find out how they all were.

'We're fine', said Trisha. 'Believe it or not, Harry's asleep. I just hope he goes through the night. I've been so tired today, you wouldn't believe it.'

Trisha's life, like many of ours, is busy and pressurized. What she doesn't realize is that her diet is probably contributing to her feelings of tiredness and preventing her from operating at her optimum level.

A varied and well-balance diet is vital to healthy, stress-free living. The food we eat determines how our bodies and minds function. When we are under stress, many of the foods we turn to for comfort or an instant lift are, in fact, stress-inducing. Trisha doesn't eat a great deal over the course of a day, but her diet of sugar and caffeine and its lack of vitamins and fibre is actually adding to her tiredness and stress and may, in the long run, damage her general health.

Exercise 80

Every day for a week, note exactly what you eat and drink.

Sunday ....

Monday ....

Tuesday ....

Wednesday ....

Thursday ....

Friday ....

Saturday ....

Study sheet 18

Paying attention to *what* and *how* you eat is one of the most positive steps you can take to protect your body, strengthening its defences against stress. If you eat too much, too little or the wrong type of food you weaken your resistance to stress, but, by making some changes in your diet, you can make your body stronger and increase your physical and mental energy.

Stress inducers

One of these is refined and processed food. If you haven't eaten for a few hours and feel weak and headachy, it's because your glucose or blood sugar level has dropped too low. You need to eat to raise it again. If what you eat at these times is refined food — like chocolate or doughnuts or white bread, which contain little fibre and few nutrients — your body doesn't have to work hard to break it down. Sugar is released too quickly. You get a rapid surge of energy as the body races to lower its blood sugar levels, but it is short-lived, and soon plummets again.

   Another stress inducer is caffeine

- 1 cup of instant coffee = 184 mg of caffeine

- 1 cup of percolated coffee = 192 mg of caffeine
- 1 cup of tea = 48–72 mg of caffeine
- 1 cola drink = 27–54 mg caffeine

A dose of 400 mg of caffeine can double your adrenalin rate. This may be at a time when your body is trying to do the same thing in response to stress. Caffeine can make you sleep less efficiently. An excess of it can aggravate stomach conditions. When you are under stress, the stomach and digestive system shut down so food and drink stay in the stomach longer. In these circumstances, caffeine can do even more harm to the stomach lining than when you are in a relaxed state.

Sugar and salt can also induce stress. As we have seen, sugar gives an instant 'high' as it floods into the bloodstream, but its effect is short-lived. Regular, excessive sugar intake makes the blood sugar level in your blood erratic and can lead to tiredness and depression.

Too much salt can lead to high blood pressure and stimulate stress arousal. The Chinese related diet to state of mind and developed the macrobiotic diet as a result. It provides an ideal balance. This balance is between yin — the female force, producing potassium — and yang — the masculine force, producing sodium — in the proportion of five parts potassium to one part sodium.

Stress reducers

One of these is unrefined complex carbohydrates. These are energy-sustaining foods, such as grains, vegetables and fruit. They provide your body with continuous energy as it breaks these substances down into fibre, nutrients and simple sugars, resulting in a steady release of energy. Your blood sugar remains stable and your appetite is naturally regulated.

Vitamins and minerals also reduce stress. The B vitamins are particularly important as they are depleted by stress. Vitamin C is also essential for stress-proofing your body. Although most of the essential vitamins and minerals are found in food, many of them are easily destroyed as a result of processing, being exposed to light, heat, overcooking and so on. Many good supplements are available.

Fibre is a stress-reducer, too. Fibre is the components of plant cells and walls that are not broken down by digestive enzymes. Foods rich in fibre, such as wholemeal bread, pasta and pulses, satisfy your hunger for longer, help to stabilize your blood sugar, sustain energy and detoxify your body.

An action plan

Replace refined carbohydrates, like white bread, biscuits and cakes, with unrefined complex carbohydrates, such as potatoes, beans and pulses.

Replace refined sugar with fresh fruit. Don't add sugar to food. Cut down on salt in cooking and at the table. Avoid products with added sugar and salt.

Eat some fibre-rich food every day. Choose from beans, pulses, vegetables and fruit with the skin left on.

Drink lots of water. Replace caffeinated drinks with herbal teas, decaffeinated coffee, caffeine-free soft drinks, fresh fruit juices, spring and mineral water.

Exercise 81

Using the above guide, think about alterations you could make to your diet. Look back at the answers you gave in Exercise 79 and note any changes that you could make without drastically reorganizing your life.

Changes I could make are ....

....

Good habits I could develop are ....

....

Bad habits I could break are ....

....

Every day for a week, note exactly what you eat and drink.

Sunday ....

Monday ....

Tuesday ....

Wednesday ....

Thursday ....

Friday ....

Saturday ....

Balance and stability

People who are mentally healthy and can meet pressure and demands with resilience and perhaps even relish, have a sense of balance in their lives. They have a variety of sources of pleasure and gratification so they can find pleasure in different ways, and if one source is taken away, they haven't lost all their resources. As we saw earlier, if you invest too much of yourself in one area — in work, for example — you leave yourself with little to fall back on, making yourself vulnerable. Paying attention to all the different areas of your life and keeping a sense of balance and variety will greatly increase your ability to cope with pressure *and* enhance the overall quality of your life.

Exercise 82

Look at the different areas of your life (family, friends, leisure, etc). List them below.

Now, go back through your list and, beside each one, write down one way in which you can affirm the importance of this area of your life. It may be that you have listed an aspect of your life you *feel* is important but, in fact, don't devote any time to it. Commit yourself now to developing areas you may have neglected.

Next, think about the opportunities for balance in your activities. What kind of proportions of work to play, exercise to rest, and so on exist in your life? List them below. For each of the headings, consider how much time you devote to the area, the priority it has and the satisfaction you derive from it.

Work   Leisure

Challenge   Ease

Exercise   Rest

If you see an imbalance, commit yourself now to making a change in your pattern of life to make it more balanced.

Exercise 83

Think about balance in the range of coping techniques at your disposal. When you are faced with problems and potentially stressful situations, do you use the same type of technique to deal with every one? Consider each of the following methods and, under each one, write down an example of when you use this method.

Tackling the problem (finding solutions, analysing, dealing with people, changing what you can change).

....

....

....

Distraction (talking to people not involved, becoming absorbed in a hobby).

....

....

Pampering yourself (taking a break, treating yourself to something).

....

....

Emotional expression (expressing your feelings, crying, shouting, creative activity like writing or music).

....

....

Try to balance your use of these methods. You may like to use what you have found out to guide you in thinking about how to create balance in your life in general, as explored in the previous exercise. If you can be flexible under stress and use a range of coping techniques, you are, in fact, likely to experience less stress because you are confident you will find answers.

Exercise 84

In the process of doing the previous exercise, you will have identified things in your life that are important to you — people, activities, and so on that are the sources of good feelings. These are your areas of stability, important bulwarks against the changes that life brings. Again, balance is important. Stability and structure in your life can be nurturing and healthy, but take care: too much, and you could become rigid and unable to adapt to change; too little, and your life lacks focus and direction. List your areas of stability below.

People ....

....

Values and beliefs ....

....

Places ....

....

Other ....

....

Other ....

....

Do you nurture and foster them? If not, think of ways you could do so. These are the most important areas of your life. These are often the ones we take for granted, assuming they will always be there, but they may not be. You may not be able to continue all your life with a sport you enjoy or in a job that gives you great satisfaction, for example. Thinking about these areas, investing time in them and planning for and anticipating possible change, will protect you from the threat of losing one of them.

Increasing and enhancing your enjoyment of life and the things that matter to you by maintaining a healthy balance in your life and being able to employ a range of strategies is an essential part of stress management.
    We all experience stress — indeed, our lives would be lessened if it were absent — but by balancing these periods of pressure with periods of recuperation, strengthening and repairing all our resources — practical, emotional, social, spiritual, creative and intellectual — will enable us to rise to the challenge of stress and cope with it.

> Stress cannot be avoided. The art is to learn how to live a full life with a minimum amount of wear and tear. The secret is . . . to live more intelligently.
>
> Hans Selye[5]

Notes

1　Hans Selye, *The Stress of Life*. New York, McGraw Hill, 1978.
2　Hans Selye, 'The general adaptation syndrome and the diseases of adaptation' in *Journal of Clinical Endocrinology* 6:117, 1946.
3　M. Friedman and R. H. Rosenman, *Type A Behaviour and Your Heart*. New York, Knopf, 1974.
4　Robert I. Woolfolk and Frank C. Richardson, *Stress, Sanity and Survival*. Souvreign Books 1978.
5　Hans Selye, *The Stress of Life*.

Index